TEACHING
PEOPLE
TEACHING
DOGS

Insights and Ideas for Instructors

DANI WEINBERG PH.D., CDBC

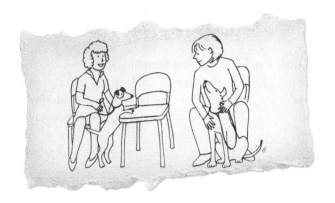

Dogwise

WENATCHEE, WASHINGTON U.S.A.

Teaching People Teaching Dogs
Insights and Ideas for Instructors
Dani Weinberg Ph.D., CDBC

Dogwise Publishing
A Division of Direct Book Service, Inc.
403 South Mission Street, Wenatchee, Washington 98801
509-663-9115, 1-800-776-2665
www.dogwisepublishing.com / info@dogwisepublishing.com

Art Director: Jon Luke
Graphic Design: Jesus Cordero, Anointing Productions
Cover and interior illustrations: Carol A. Byrnes, CPDT-KA, www.diamondsintheruff.com.

Author photograph: Joyce Fay

Limits of Liability and Disclaimer of Warranty:
The author and publisher shall not be liable in the event of incidental or consequential damages in connection with, or arising out of, the furnishing, performance, or use of the instructions and suggestions contained in this book.

ISBN: 9781617812859

Library of Congress Cataloging-in-Publication Data on file at http://www.loc.gov/publish/cip/

Printed in the U.S.A.

DEDICATION

I dedicate this book to my own German Shepherds, past and present, who have been my most forgiving teachers:
Joe, Lily, Sweetheart, Rose, Honey, Sweetie,
Ruby, Caro, Angel, Lovey, and Zia.
And to Jerry, for everything.

ACKNOWLEDGMENTS

My warm appreciation goes to Val Hughes. She was the first editor of *Forward*, the quarterly publication of NADOI (National Association of Dog Obedience Instructors). Val was an exemplary editor, encouraging and supporting me when I was a regular columnist for the journal. Without realizing it, I started working on this book in 1995 when I was asked to write a 500-word article for the first issue of *Forward*. The columns I wrote during the next six years provided the framework for this book. If you've been a *Forward* reader all these years, you might find hints and echo of those columns in these chapters, now much more developed and expanded as my own thinking and experience have grown.

My thanks to Betty Mueller, my publisher, for seeing the possibilities of the book and helping me realize them.

Several of my colleagues were kind enough to read the manuscript. I thank them for their thoughtful comments:

Barbara Brill, owner of the Aggressive Behaviors in Dogs list on the Internet (http://groups.yahoo.com/group/agbeh)

Suzanne Clothier, author of *Bones Would Rain From the Sky: Deepening Our Relationships with Dogs.*

Terry Ryan, President of Legacy Canine Behavior and Training, and author of *Coaching People To Train Their Dogs.*

Kathy Sdao, owner of Bright Spot Dog Training and Clicker Expo faculty member.

I also thank my colleagues and students here in New Mexico and around the world (thanks to the Internet) for the marvelous continuing education they provide.

A special Thank You to Dogwise for taking on the often messy job of reissuing this book. First published in 2006, the ideas have not needed updating, but it was still a lot of extra work.

Finally, to my husband, Jerry Weinberg, I offer my deepest thanks. He was my best, and most loving, critic and my inspiration.

TABLE OF CONTENTS

INTRODUCTION

"On the third day I had an epiphany:
the behavior of dogs is predictable."

Inspired Instructing

Have you ever wondered what it would feel like to be captured by aliens? I've actually had that experience. Well, not exactly by aliens, but by a different species called Dog. And not exactly captured, but captivated. It happened in the mountains of Colorado. I was attending a 5-day workshop about Conflict Resolution. On the third day, we were asked to refrain from speaking or using language in any other way (like writing notes) for the entire day. That was probably the most memorable day of the week for me—not just because of the marvelous lesson in communication, but also because of a particular moment of communication that I will never forget.

I was doing very well at following the no-speaking rule and even enjoying the silence—until the group went on a hike. We climbed a steep slope that ended at a beautiful meadow. In silence, we sat on the ground, close together, taking silent pleasure in each other's company. Suddenly, the biggest and hairiest dog I had ever seen appeared at the edge of the meadow, seemingly emerging out of thin air because the trail up to the meadow was so steep that we had no warning of his arrival.

The dog saw our group immediately and was irresistibly drawn to us, rushing over to lick and nuzzle each person. When he came to me—I spoke! Out loud! I have absolutely no memory of the words I uttered but only of being transported—"captured"—into another universe. Nothing existed except the dog and me, in profound communication. I was speaking English, and he was "speaking" Dog, and the moment was one of perfect connection.

Then I felt an elbow (human) in my side and I came out of my trance, a little embarrassed at having broken the silence rule. The dog's owner finally appeared on the meadow, a slower hiker than his dog.

2

For the rest of the day and for years to come, I marvelled at what had happened. If connection was based on communication, then how could this have happened when the two participants in the dialogue were using different languages—and one of them non-verbal?

I understand now that this was a kind of magic, a moment of complete engagement between Dog and me. I also realize that I experience this magic, in small measure, whenever I am with a dog. It can be one of my own dogs or a student's dog—makes no difference. The moment is seldom as dramatic as it was that first time on a Colorado mountain, but I feel it just as deeply.

This magical connection is the beginning of what I call inspired instructing. It's about being fully present, in pure communication with a dog. My students, of course, have to learn how to do this with their own dogs, but they always recognize the magic when they see me do it. Maybe this is what they're seeing when they ask why their dogs are more attentive to me than to them. No mystery here! Inspired instructors have had lots of experience making immediate connections with new dogs. An important part of my job is to show my students that they can do this too. Once the magic is there with their own dogs, anything is possible. I have seen truly amazing turnarounds in dog behavior when the dog-person relationship was infused with real communication.

I also want to have this kind of communication with my human students. The person-to-person form of this magic is called empathy, and it comes from having had many of the same experiences that my students are now having and remembering how I felt. I know about the sleep-deprived desperation that makes me think of returning a puppy to the breeder. I know about the fury that once, many years ago, made me slap a dog on the face. (I still shudder that I was able to do this.) I know about the grief and emptiness of losing a dog.

I also know about the thrill of qualifying in an obedience trial for the first time ever, the pleasure of hiking with dogs and seeing the world through their eyes (and noses), and the transcendent joy of watching my dogs play exuberantly with each other.

When we connect empathically with our human students, we can teach them how to connect magically with their dogs. That's inspired instructing, and that's what this book is about.

About This Book

This book is about the dog-training instructor's first job: teaching people. Although we describe ourselves as "dog trainers," we know that our human students require much more attention and understanding than do their canines. If we don't inspire their interest and cooperation, they will not be successful in training their dogs.

The primary message of this book is that we are teaching people first, rather than training dogs. This book is not a comprehensive work on how to be an instructor, but it will contribute to your becoming a great instructor. Nor is the book a how-to manual that gives detailed directions for teaching specific behaviors, but it will make your training instructions more effective. And if you're training your own dog, this book will enhance your efforts by suggesting new ways to think about the teaching and learning process.

But that's not enough. We instructors are people too. In order to do our best teaching, we must take our own humanity into account. We must constantly examine what we're doing and why. I learned how to do this from Virginia Satir, family therapist extraordinaire, who was a major influence on my life and work.

Virginia believed we have within us the resources we need to live happy and productive lives. Sometimes, though, we need help to develop our skills so that we can actually use our inner resources to best advantage.

One of Virginia's great strengths was her ability to choose an approach to help a client and, if it didn't seem to be working, to change course immediately, without any embarrassment or apology. She would actually say to the client "Okay then, let's try this instead." That's what this book is for: helping you open your mind to new ideas, consider other views, and explore new possibilities in your instructing.

This book offers you information, insights, and ideas to help you work more effectively with your human students. It urges you to engage your intelligence and curiosity and courage to try some of these ideas in your own classes and private lessons. Virginia used to put it this way: "Taste everything, but swallow only what fits for you."

Every outstanding instructor I know is also a lifelong student, constantly seeking new ideas to taste. As instructors, then, we have a lot in common with the people who come to our classes with their dogs. Above all, we share the dream of building the most satisfying relationships possible between people and their dogs. This book will help you and your students realize that dream.

How I Became An Instructor

Never in my wildest dreams did I imagine that I would, one day, be living with dogs, let alone have a career as a professional dog trainer and instructor.

I was raised by professional-class European parents to be highly cultivated (read "marriageable"). When I was 5 years old, I started taking piano lessons. When I was 10, ballet lessons were added, because my mother thought it would make me thinner and more graceful. I also took private French lessons, studied Spanish and Russian in school, and made several summer trips to Europe during my college years. After college, I continued living at home and found an "interesting" job, quite unrelated to my education or career dreams, while presumably waiting to find a suitable husband.

These were the things that well-bred New York City girls of my generation were supposed to do. We were well educated, usually in the humanities (more "ladylike" than the sciences). After graduation, we worked at respectable but low-paying jobs for a couple of years. Then, we met and married Mr. Right (my parents were sure that he would be Dr. Right, like my father). We set up house in an apartment not far from where our parents lived and, as soon as we were able to start a family, we quit our jobs to become full-time "homemakers."

Most of my friends lived up to these expectations, but I was something of a disappointment to my parents. I turned down several eligible young doctors, waited until I met a man from Chicago of all places, married him when I was 25, and promptly left town for the Wild West (Michigan).

My family had come to America as refugees at the beginning of World War II. We lived in a Manhattan apartment in New York City. I don't believe that any of my friends had pets. It never occurred to me to want a dog. One summer, I did buy some goldfish at the local five-and-dime store, but they didn't last much longer than other living things last in Manhattan. Only the cockroaches seemed to thrive.

Instead of having dogs, we kids entertained ourselves on the city streets. Bikes and roller skates were hardly practical or safe in that environment. Instead, we played hopscotch, handball against the walls of apartment buildings, and hide and seek using the basements of apartment buildings as our hiding places.

I was not one of those animal-loving children who dreams of having a dog or owning a horse. For the first 33 years of my life, in fact, I was oblivious to the existence of non-human animals. Somewhere along the way, I realized that I was deathly afraid of dogs.

I don't recall ever having been frightened or attacked by a dog. I suspect that my fear was something I learned from my mother. She told me that, as a child, she had had a dog—a Spitz. Years later, my mother, now a married woman with a young child, had to leave her home on 24-hours notice. She left behind everything she knew and loved, and we came to America. I believe that she simply never wanted to set herself up again for another painful loss, so she never had another dog.

I found my way into Anthropology. I went to graduate school, did my doctoral research, taught at the university for many years, and, along the way, became a Professor. During those years, I never gave a single thought to having a dog.

My first conscious and mindful encounter with a dog happened when I was 33 years old and met Heidi, a German Shepherd. Although she had a beautiful face and a sweet temperament, she would never be a breed champion because her color, a lovely golden tan, was "wrong," according to the breed standard. I doubt that she was even registered with the American Kennel Club.

Heidi belonged to our neighbors across the street, and her life was idyllic. She spent her days running freely in the neighborhood, doing rounds with the postman, playing with the neighborhood kids, and going home for meals and more love from her owners. I generally avoided her. She was a dog, after all, and I was afraid of dogs.

One Easter, our neighbors were going to be out of town. They had made arrangements for someone else to come in and feed Heidi. They asked us if we could just keep an eye on her while they were gone for the week. That was the week that I began my love affair with dogs.

We opened our house to Heidi. At first, when she came to visit us, 1 was apprehensive and watchful, half expecting that she would destroy something, or pee on the carpet. Maybe even bite me. On the third day, I had an epiphany.

As usual, I was watching Heidi carefully. She was taking her morning nap on the floor of our sunroom when a large spider walked by. Immediately awake and alert, Heidi stalked the spider, following it across the room and under the piano. Then, bored with her new toy, she pounced on the spider—and it was gone! The entire event lasted no longer than 30 seconds, but, in that brief time, as I watched Heidi and the spider, it suddenly came to me: *the behavior of dogs is predictable.* And if it's predictable, that means that all I had to do was watch and learn, and I would never be hurt by a dog.

Apparently, somewhere in the part of my subconscious mind that builds models, I had been classifying dogs under the heading "Wild Animals." What amuses me so much about this today is that I must have also thought, at that time, that the behavior of wild animals was not predictable. I had somehow glossed "wild" into "unpredictable" (as I think many people do).

That was the beginning of the end of my fear of dogs. Several years later, when we were living on a farm in Nebraska, we were offered a German Shepherd who was a "child of divorce" (my sister-in-law's). I happily joined my husband in accepting. Joe Pickle was the first in our succession of German Shepherds. He had been bom in a barn, the result of a backyard breeding. He turned out to be one of those dogs that is the exception to the rule. Even though bred casually by uninformed owners, Joe was as beautiful as any German Shepherd Champion. He was huge, weighing 110 pounds, and one of the sweetest and most gentle dogs of any breed that I've ever known.

After a few months of watching Joe loll around the farm, we decided he was lonely, so we bought our second German Shepherd with the $25 that my mother had sent us for our anniversary. How do you buy a dog? Why, you look at the ads in the paper, of course, and then you go and look at the dog, and if you like what you see (or the dog "chooses" you), you take that dog home. At least, that was what I believed at the time.

Lily, 4 months old then, was one of two remaining puppies in a backyard-bred litter. She was the runt of her litter, the last one to be sold, the one no one else wanted. At that time, I knew nothing about backyard breeders, German Shepherds, behavior, or training. But I loved her with a passion. She was my first very-own dog.

Lily and her brother had never been outside their yard or met any strangers, human or canine. She was definitely a German Shepherd, although blond all over. We paid our money and put her in the car for the short drive home, during which she trembled and vomited the entire way. Her ears remained plastered flat against her head for several days. She must have been absolutely terrified. Still, though, the first thing she did when we got home was to bark furiously at Joe. Very quickly, they became best friends.

I thought it would be fun to take Lily to Obedience School. I realize now that "fun" is hardly ever the reason that people take their dogs to class. More likely, they're having problems and feel helpless about how to solve them. I was, however, happily innocent. Joe and Lily were outside dogs. They never left our 5-acre farm. They had no experience with the rest of the world. There were no problems. We even had a mobile vet who drove out to our place whenever the dogs needed their shots or had some other medical issues.

Training Lily turned out not to be so much fun. The first problem was to get her there. She had never been in a car until the day she came home with us. For the first year we had her, she threw up regularly on rides and fought us whenever we tried to put her into the car. So every Thursday evening, I'd start our trip to class a half hour early, coaxing and dragging her into the car. By the time we arrived there, we were both exhausted and spent a lot of class time huddled together on the floor.

I didn't know my instructor's name for the first four weeks, and she certainly didn't know mine or my dog's. That wasn't so bad during those early weeks when the class was doing everything together. But when we started learning the Recall and working individually, it would be: "The Shepherd. Call your dog."

I never saw my instructor smile. In fact, I don't recall that we ever made eye contact with each other. 1 never heard her praise anyone in the class, human or canine. I do remember, though, the sarcastic, biting remarks she would toss at me (and other students) when I made a "mistake" of some kind. "Look at her, treating her dog like a marshmallow!" I also remember the general atmosphere of blame and my feelings of being wrong, stupid, uncoordinated, and incompetent.

Only my indomitable stubbornness kept me going. At the time, I never dreamed that someday I'd be teaching my own obedience classes. Now, so many years later, I cherish those first 10 weeks of my life in dogs because they taught me what not to do.

For some obscure reason, 1 decided to enter Lily in a local obedience trial—never having even seen one before. We were both so nervous on the drive to the show site that Lily vomited several times in the back seat of my Volkswagen Bug. Yes indeed! She was most definitely a German Shepherd and as handler-sensitive as they come!

PetsMart® and the other super-stores had not yet come into being. The pet industry offered us not much more than dog food and toys at that time. And if you had to take your dog somewhere, she just rode in the back seat of your car. So Lily was neither crated nor seat-belted but just riding loose.

The trial was, as you might expect, a total disaster—though I was thrilled that Lily came to me on the Recall, since that had always been a difficult exercise for us. When we did our off-leash Heeling, she followed me, about 4 feet behind, with her head down and her tail tucked between her legs. The judge asked me if I beat her, and I think now that he was not just joking. No one had ever told me that you had to teach a dog to heel off leash. I thought it was just something that happened magically, once the dog knew how to heel on leash.

Because training was so unpleasant (following the instructions of our obedience class instructor) and the trial such a miserable experience, I gave up on what I thought of as "training" for a few years. Somehow, though, I must have continued training, because both Joe and Lily, and eventually the two puppies we kept out of their litter, were very biddable and well-behaved dogs. (Not knowing any better, we became backyard breeders ourselves.) Maybe for this reason, friends began to ask me for help with their dogs. And though I didn't know it at the time, that was the beginning of my career as an instructor.

Then, one day, I went to an obedience trial—just to watch—and sat transfixed near the Utility ring. I remember watching dogs do Scent Discrimination, marvelling at this seemingly impossible exercise, and dreaming that someday I would have a dog who could do that. And now I do! In fact, I have two dogs who are world-class at this exercise, and a third, my four- month-old puppy, well on his way.

Over the years, as I studied and trained other dogs, I learned to speak Dog-As-a-Second-Language. For a long time, though, I felt quite inadequate, compared with all those people who had grown up with dogs and who, 1 imagined, had thereby become fluent in Dog. I now realize that, in some ways, 1 probably know more about dogs than they do, in the same way that I know more about English grammar (my second language) than most native speakers. I had to learn English the hard way, rather than absorbing it naturally from birth.

In 1989, about 14 years after getting Lily, I started teaching dog-training classes. As university professors, my husband and I had our summers free, and we used to spend them in a small mountain town in Colorado. I presented myself to the local rescue organization that consisted of half a dozen women who were trying to make up for the lack of a real animal shelter in the county. I offered to teach classes for them. Apparently, there had been, once before, an obedience trainer in town for a short time, but she was long gone.

Two of the women in this rescue group had, amazingly, trained their dogs to the Utility Dog title, the most advanced in competition obedience, working entirely from books, with no live instruction or coaching. Their primary concern now, though, was to teach people just the bare basics of responsible dog ownership so as to reduce the population of intact, unsocialized dogs that were often just dumped when they reached adolescence and starting to cause trouble. They were thrilled to have someone like me, and I was thrilled, as always, at the opportunity to teach.

During those years in Colorado, I taught both puppy and adult-dog classes. My classes were definitely of the "general public" variety. My students spanned a huge slice of rural humanity, including a cashier at the supermarket, students at the local college, attorneys and judges, housewives, grade-school kids, men who had acquired their dogs solely for hunting, and a retired and hearing-impaired rancher who used a long and frayed rope as a leash. It was a rich and sometimes frustrating experience, but most definitely a learning experience. This is where I cut my teeth as an instructor.

By this time, I had gotten serious about training and competing with my own dogs. I had started attending seminars and camps and was going for total immersion—reading everything I could, practicing on my own dogs, and trying to become a better trainer.

My skills as a teacher of people had always been excellent, and I was a favorite professor among students at the university. After a couple of years of teaching my dog-training classes, I began to chafe at an incongruity between how I taught my students at the university and how I trained dogs. At the university, I was involved in a special program for freshmen that was based on the idea that people learn best if they're allowed to figure things out for themselves. This learner-centered program was designed to create an environment in which students could wrestle with the real world and, through that struggle, come to their own understanding of how to solve problems. The teacher was simply a guide, while the students themselves drove the learning process.

When I was training dogs, however, I was doing most of the work. Instead of encouraging the dogs to be active learners and to drive the learning process, I was caught up in the traditional model of dog training. My job, as I saw it then, was to train a dog by showing and telling and physically manipulating it to do what I wanted. If that worked and the dog learned, I took the credit. If the dog didn't learn, I blamed the dog, instead of turning the spotlight on myself and my training methods. This approach worked pretty well for many dogs but dismally for others. And for those others, their owners became discouraged and angry and felt guilty and inadequate. This was not working!

I began the gradual shift away from traditional training— also, appropriately, called "command-based training"—and towards operant training. Instead of teaching by telling, I began to train dogs by enabling them to learn for themselves. All I had to do was supply a positive consequence to the behavior I wanted and no response to the behaviors I didn't want. That makes it sound easy—but it wasn't! After all, I grew up and was educated in a culture that tells us "we learn from our mistakes" and inculcates in us a "no pain-no gain" philosophy. Our culture waggles a warning finger at us and reminds us that learning is hard and serious work and that, if we're having fun, we can't be learning. I have had to work hard to arrive at a "Catch 'Em Doing It Right" approach. And I still have my moments of backsliding, but at least I recognize them more quickly now.

Since 1993, I've been an exclusively clicker trainer—using mostly positive reinforcement, infrequently negative punishment, and a marker signal (the clicker) to let the dog know instantly which response would be reinforced with something the dog likes. I'm now deeply satisfied that how I train dogs is also how I teach people. In fact, I am so convinced that these two teaching contexts can and should be identical that, when friends from my former life as an anthropologist ask me what I do, I tell them that I do exactly what I've been doing all my life. I teach people how to enhance their communication skills and build stronger, happier relationships. The only difference—and I see it as an insignificant one—is that these skills and knowledge are now applied to their relationships with their dogs. I've observed, too, that "practicing" on our dogs makes us better with people.

I now understand how devoted my students are to their dogs, whether model canine citizens or bratty out-of-control delinquents. I make a point of knowing the names of my students (both canine and human) and also something about who they are and what's important to them. For example, was this dog rescued from an abusive home? Or is the family now in crisis, such as illness or divorce? Or is the 11-year-old handler a little shy and low on self-esteem? Many of my students are not as resilient and forgiving as I was when I took Lily to obedience school. I want to make sure that their first obedience class is not their last.

This book brings together my two greatest passions: people and dogs. You will probably learn more, in reading this book, about the people side of it—about your students, if you're an instructor, and about yourself—and that's fine because that's what I think training dogs is all about.

Recommended Reading

Alexander, Melissa

   2003   Click For Joy! Questions and Answers from Clicker Trainers and their Dogs.

   Beautifully written and full of substance, this is an excellent book for anyone interested in doing or teaching clicker training.

PART ONE: THE STUDENT

*"When we connect empathically with our
human students, we can teach them
how to connect magically with their dogs."*

Part One: The Student

This book is divided into two sections, each focusing on one of the key human players in the dog-training game: the student, and the instructor. Here's a brief summary of what to expect in Part One, The Student.

Chapter 1 describes the most fundamental learning objectives I have for my students. For example, they need to know that their dogs are capable of learning, or we won't get very far trying to teach the dogs how to sit on cue. My students also need to know that a dog's behavior might be perfectly normal even if objectionable, that dogs do have emotions, and that good training is fun and not a chore.

Chapter 2 corrects some of the mistaken assumptions students hold about the nature of dogs and how to live with them. I know about these mistaken assumptions intimately from my own "Dark Ages" as a dog owner.

Chapter 3 reveals a deeper level of unconscious beliefs that students hold about their own dogs. Bringing these beliefs to awareness makes dog training much simpler and more successful.

Chapter 4 discusses one of the most troublesome of these beliefs—that dogs are like people. Rather than declaring anthropomorphism a taboo, as is often done, we can teach our students when this point of view is actually useful.

Chapter 5 offers an alternative way to understand and work with students who are sometimes labeled as "difficult"—so that we don't simply dismiss them as being hopelessly beyond our reach.

Finally, Chapter 6 shows how to improve the dynamics of communication between instructor and student.

CHAPTER 1
What I Want My Students to Learn

My office is an even bigger mess than usual these days as I prepare for my next series of classes. No matter how many books I read on getting organized, my filing system remains the same: piles of papers, placed and arranged in ways that only I understand.

As I look around now, I see a pile of e-mail messages and articles I've saved that contain new teaching ideas. There's a copy of my old class manual, along with the copying masters, waiting for revision since I can't seem to use the same set of articles and handouts twice in a row. There's a pile of last year's class outlines and homework sheets, marked up with notes for changes to be made. There's a pile of 3-ring folders for the new class manual. There's a pile of work aprons that I give to my students as bait bags, and a pile of waist leashes for my students. I can no longer see the top of my desk. And I'm feeling both excited and overwhelmed.

Before I can make any sense of all this chaos, I have to go "back to school" myself—back to basics—and I ask myself: What do I want my students to learn? I'm not talking about what the dogs will learn but what the humans, at the other end of the leash, will come away with. Because I know that it's the people I'm really teaching.

18

It's easy to design a training plan to teach a dog to walk nicely on a loose leash. The real challenge for instructors is teaching the people and not training the dogs. Everything we can do to help people understand principles and build their skills will benefit the dogs and their training. So I do a lot of rethinking, redesigning, rewriting, and, most important, reaffirming for myself what are the important goals I have for my human students.

My Dog Can Learn

One of my greatest pleasures in teaching is to watch a student's eyes grow huge as she realizes that "My dog can learn!" When I first meet a new student, I spend a few minutes working with the dog—both to get a sense of who this dog is and also to start this transformation in the owner's mind. I might do a quick lesson in sitting, or walking on a loose leash, or simply looking at me. Any good trainer can accomplish some training in five minutes. What's so nice about operant training, though, is that the owner can see the dog making choices and can actually watch the learning happening.

Then I give the student a handful of treats and say "Now you try it." And they can do it! That's the second transformation in the student's mind. Not only is my dog educable, but I can actually train a behavior!

As soon as students start to believe that their dogs can learn and that they can teach them, some wonderful things happen. First, hope replaces resignation or even despair. If I can teach my dog to sit, then maybe I can even teach him to stop jumping on me. Behavior problems become training challenges and opportunities.

Second, the student begins to see her dog as a lovable and unique individual, rather than a stubborn and spiteful creature who lies awake at night thinking of ways to annoy the family.

She begins to understand that most behaviors are learned—or not learned. If my dog doesn't always come when I call him, then maybe that's because I haven't taught him how to do that.

What's Normal?

That's a good question! Instructors know that dogs are members of a different species. Our students, though, sometimes forget that. Behaviors that they find "impolite" or even repulsive are often entirely normal canine behaviors. The top three of these behaviors that come to mind immediately are eating horse poop (and other unmentionables), licking one's private parts in public (or anywhere else, for that matter), and mounting Aunt Sarah's leg.

Animal behaviorists seem to be in disagreement on this question. Is there such a thing as "normal," or should we speak only of "adaptive" behaviors—those that optimize survival? What about the role of environment in behavior? If a dog does something "abnormal," is that because of external circumstances or internal pathology? Or maybe we can consider only the excesses or deficits as "abnormal" behavior. But then, how do we measure "excess" and "deficit"? In other words, when is barking excessive, and when is a dog showing insufficient bonding with the owner?

These are hard questions. To simplify the issue, I like to think about behavior as being either desired or undesired by us humans. Eating horse poop might be highly adaptive, functional, and normal—but neither my students nor I want our dogs to do it.

Steven Lindsay, in his excellent book *Applied Dog Behavior and Training, Volume Two,* presents a Dog Ethogram—"an orderly compilation of what a dog does" (p.39-42). Just a few items on the list are: Affiliative Behavior (activities relating to the

20

human-dog bond, such as separation distress, attention seeking, following, cooperative behavior), Appetitive Behavior (everything related to getting food and eating it), Play (of all kinds, ranging from social to sexual to predatory), and Exploratory Behavior (including some of our favorites, such as sniffing, digging, chewing, and scent rolling).

Most of the behavior categories listed on the ethogram describe what we love about our dogs. Some, though, are species-specific and not on our own human list of Desired Behaviors. And each behavior category comes with its own excesses and deficits.

Once our students understand that these are simply the things that dogs do, they can drop their judgmental attitudes and begin to make rational decisions. Instead of thinking in terms of normal and abnormal, they can ask the simple question: Do I want this behavior or not? And, if not, then what can I do to change it?

Dogs Are Not People

Many of my students have a hard time with this one. Not only are dogs members of a different biological species but they also participate in a very different kind of communication system from our own. Dogs are not linguistic creatures. Instead, they're fantastically capable readers of body language and emotion. And that's where people get into trouble.

"He doesn't listen" is a common complaint. Yes he does! But what he "hears" is not necessarily what you told him in words. Instead, he responds to tone of voice, posture, facial expression, and all the other clues to the emotions leaking through those words.

One of the classic examples of miscommunication is the case of the man whose dog has been soiling in the house. This gentleman comes home from work and is greeted by his "guilty" dog who "knows he did something bad" (probably another accident, the owner thinks). The dog is averting his eyes and cowering. The owner's annoyance at his "bad" dog increases, and he screams at the dog. The dog cowers even more and finally runs to hide under the bed.

I want my students to understand that this dog is behaving respectfully and, upon sensing the owner's displeasure, starts to show "calming signals" as a way to appease him. That's just how dogs do it! In order to avoid conflict and confrontation, they turn away, they scratch, they yawn, they sit or lie down. And if that doesn't work, then the fight-or-flight mechanism takes over—as it did with this dog who simply ran away, terrified.

Sometimes I think that this elementary behavioral training is much more important for my students than all my instruction on how to teach a dog to perform basic behaviors. If students can learn to observe their dogs dispassionately and learn what behaviors mean in dog "language," their relationships will be based more solidly on reality and connection.

Dogs Have Emotions

Yes, they do! The problem is that we have no idea what's going on inside the dog when she's having an emotion. All we know is what we can see on the outside. And that's probably just as true for humans, as anyone knows who has ever misinterpreted the meaning behind another person's behavior.

When we communicate with dogs, in the absence of a common language, the first thing we can do is train ourselves to be excellent observers. Just as they watch us carefully, so do we have to watch them. I work hard to teach my students what to look at and for.

I also teach my students that dogs cannot learn when they are experiencing strong emotions like fear or agitation. (Nor can humans, for that matter.) As the dog becomes more and more uncertain and worried, the handler's frustration also mounts. Then we have not one but two animals that are in no condition to learn anything.

Bob Bailey, the master animal trainer, draws on his many years of experience and reminds us that "Pavlov is always sitting on your shoulder." We can be training up a storm but if the dog has shifted into that part of the central nervous system that expresses strong emotion, we might as well quit for the day. There's a fundamental incompatibility between those classically-conditioned (Pavlovian) emotional responses and the operant behavior that we want in a training session.

We've all seen this in our classes, especially on the first night. There will be a dog that seems to be in a trance—completely unresponsive, unwilling to take food treats, unable even to look at her owner, and just wanting to disappear behind the owner's chair. That dog is experiencing a conditioned emotional response. It doesn't matter what we call the emotion, and it doesn't matter when or how it was conditioned. All that matters is that the dog is incapable of being psychologically present and learning. What to do? Sometimes I move the team further away from the group, hoping that this will reduce the dog's anxiety. Or I might show the owner how to get food into the dog's mouth in a non-forceful way so that the dog has to start eating, thereby moving out of that emotional state and becoming mentally functional.

Some Basics of Training

I want my students to understand some of the basic principles of how to change behavior. One of these is the difference between training and management. When we're training, we're trying to change the behavior of the dog directly. When we're managing, we're changing behavior indirectly by changing the environment. So, for example, we can train a dog to stay within the boundaries of our property, or we can manage the situation by building a wall. The art of changing behavior is knowing when to do which of these.

A couple recently came to see me with a 3 month old puppy they had just adopted. "She keeps getting into the trash", they complained. Trying hard to keep a straight face, I suggested that they put covers on their trash cans or, if that wasn't possible, put the trash cans high up on counters that the puppy couldn't reach. They looked at each other in amazement and said "Why, that's brilliant!" I graciously accepted their praise for my genius, knowing full well that it was simply not worthwhile to try to train a puppy to stay out of the trash when a little management would solve the problem immediately.

Another basic principle I want my students to understand is what's sometimes called the "Dead Dog Rule". This Rule says that anything a dead dog can do is not a behavior and, therefore, cannot be trained. For example, can a dead dog not jump on people? Of course! How, then, can we get a living dog to "stop" jumping on people? If we approach the problem this way, we're making it much harder than it needs to be.

Human psychologists talk about the "embedded message". Here's an example. What happens if I say to you "Please don't think of a hippopotamus"? Chances are, you'll immediately form a mental picture of a hippopotamus! You don't hear the "don't" part of the instruction. If, however, I say to you "Please think of a rabbit", then you can easily do that.

So when we want to get rid of an undesired behavior, we have to think affirmatively. I ask my students "What do you want your dog to do instead of jumping on people?" They can usually think of several good alternatives—sit, lie down, come back to me. These are all legitimate, "live dog" behaviors that are incompatible with jumping and that can be trained and earn rewards for the dog every time. For example, if the dog is trained to Sit for Greeting, then the approaching person will always come and pet the dog. I want my students to begin thinking about what they want their dogs to do, rather than not do.

I also want to help my students with the logistics of training: when and where to train, for how long, how often, and when to stop. When I first started taking my own dogs to obedience school, back in the 1970s, we were told that we had to train for 30 minutes every day. And that was all we were told. I remember torturing myself and my first dog with 30-minute long sessions in the garage that I imagined had something to do with "training." We repeated behaviors endlessly. We both became increasingly frustrated, I often returned to the house in tears. And my dog didn't learn a thing—except maybe that "training" was about as bad as going to the vet.

I hope I've made my students' lot easier than mine was. I give them specific instructions on how to run a training session. I've experimented with various devices to help them keep up with their daily training—like a grid to post on the fridge that lists all the behaviors they need to work on that week and allows them to check off each one, every day. I tell them when to train in a quiet undisturbed place, and when and how to start introducing environmental distractions. I suggest that they use a kitchen timer so that they remember to keep their training sessions short and sweet. I let them know when it's time to start training "naked"— with no treats on their person but only on a nearby table. I show them how to make non-food reinforcers just as highly valued as food. In other words, I see it as part of my job to teach my students about the mechanics, and not just the principles, of good training.

Training is Fun

My greatest hope as an instructor is communicating to my students how much fun it is to train a dog. Training should not be a chore but a pleasure. If it's more like work than fun, then something is wrong.

Our human students need at least as much positive reinforcement as do their dogs. They begin to get it almost immediately when they realize that they're doing much more than just teaching their dogs how to sit on cue. Training is about building a stronger and more loving relationship with a dog. It's about getting to know a dog in a more intimate way than ever before. It's about watching this marvelous alien being learning new things and delighting in the ever-expanding boundaries of his brain and his heart. It's no wonder that our students describe their dogs as their "best friends."

And, to take a more pragmatic view, training seems to have strong carryover effects that go far beyond learning specific behaviors. Many people take their dogs to obedience class in order to have better "control" over them. What they discover, though, is that, instead of control, they now have better communication with their dogs.

Instead of trying to contain and control their dogs, I want my students to begin looking for more activities that they can do together—hiking, travel, visiting friends (both human and canine), engaging in dog sports, earning titles like the Canine Good Citizen, and sharing their dogs with people in healthcare facilities.

Finally, I want my students to be inspired to continue training after our class ends. I want them to see that dogs, like people and all living beings, are enriched by lifelong learning. I want them to think of the end of our few weeks together as just a beginning.

Recommended Reading and Viewing

Bailey, Bob

Bob and the late Marian Breland Bailey published papers and produced videos but never put together any books. A good way to start exploring their work is by visiting their website: <http://www.hsnp.com/behavior>

Lindsay, Steven R.

2000 Handbook of Applied Dog Behavior and Training. Volume 1: Adaptation and Learning.

This monumental work is not bedside reading, but it's important for the education of every serious dog trainer and instructor. Volume One begins with a discussion of "Origins and Domestication," moves through chapters on behavior, biology and neurobiology of behavior, classical and operant conditioning, aversive control of behavior, learning and behavior disorders, and, finally, a discussion of the cultural and psychological ramifications of the human-animal bond.

2001 Handbook of Applied Dog Behavior and Training. Volume 2: Etiology and Assessment.

Volume Two covers the history of applied dog behavior and training; behavioral assessment; fears and phobias; attachment, separation, and related disorders; excessive behavior; aggressive behavior; intraspecific and territorial aggression; social competition; and appetite and elimination problems.

Gorwitz-Kalnajs, Sarah

2006   The Language of Dogs, (set of 2 DVDs)

An excellent presentation of the non-verbal "language of dogs" and what their signals tell us. This is a well-edited video version of Kalnajs' seminar in which she provides multiple examples of each signal, showing different dogs. Suitable for both instructors and their students.

Rugaas, Turid

1997   On Talking Terms with Dogs: Calming Signals.

A small book containing invaluable information about how dogs communicate and, by extension, how we can communicate better with them.

2005   Calming Signals: What Your Dog Tells You. (DVD)

This is the companion DVD to Turid Rugaas's book. Well worth watching.

CHAPTER 2
Ten Assumptions That Lead Students Astray

If you're like me, you're probably happy to forget your early years of dog training. I blush at some of the silly ideas and beliefs I had in the Dark Ages. But when I work with a beginning student, it all comes back to me. Why, they have the same silly ideas and beliefs that I had!

Embarrassing as it is to remember my own ignorance, I'm grateful for those memories because they help me help my students today. So, here comes a nice deep breath—and I will reveal some of my ideas from the Dark Ages.

1. If you own two dogs that you love, you should breed them to each other so that you'll have more of these wonderful dogs.

Never mind that you know nothing about their genetic background because they were born in someone's barn. Our two wonderful German Shepherds, Joe and Lily, produced a litter of seven puppies. We kept two of them. One developed severe hip dysplasia at 11 months, endured a total hip replacement at 10 years, then died two years later after a protracted case of pancreatic cancer. Her littermate and their mother both died of hemangiosarcoma at the age of 10. It's no wonder that I'm now an ardent proponent of letting the professionals do the breeding. I now believe that the only good reason to breed dogs is to contribute to improving the overall quality of that breed.

2. If you live in the country, your dogs should run free so that they can be "free spirits" in their "natural" environment.

I did not know that country dogs have a life span of about 3 years and that they most often die violently, hit by trucks and farm vehicles. I also did not understand that dogs are a highly domesticated species—so far from a "natural" canid state that it's laughable. A few years ago, I was privileged to attend a workshop at Wolf Park, the wolf research facility in Indiana. After three days immersed in wolf behavior, I returned home and was greeted at the door by my two German Shepherds. That moment provided me with the greatest single learning of the workshop: dogs are not wolves.

Dogs have been selected and bred for their juvenile characteristics—their cuteness of physical appearance (wide eyes, for example), their playfulness and curiosity, and their willingness to approach us. As a natural consequence, dogs are also very dependent on their human caretakers—contrary to the "Homeward Bound" movie myth. My free-ranging country dogs used to take off after deer, cross the highway to snack on a roadkill, bathe in odoriferous who-knows-what, and sometimes drag home half a rotted cow carcass they had found. But they always came home in time for dinner.

One day, our neighbor, a sheep rancher, visited and told us that some dogs had been harrassing his livestock. With a friendly smile, he informed us that he would shoot any dog he found on his property. The next day, our yard was fenced. I have since become an expert on containing dogs.

3. Anyway, dog crates are prisons, and you wouldn't want to put your "best friend" in a cage, would you?

Like so many dog owners, I was anthropomorphizing. I didn't know that dogs can learn to love their "dens." I never thought about the occasional medical need to confine an ill or recuperating dog. And I never considered the safety issues of dogs riding loose in cars.

4. But why would you ever need to take a dog anywhere away from home—except maybe to the vet's for annual shots?

What happens when a friend visits with her young children? Or when the family goes on a camping vacation with their dogs? I didn't know about the possible tragic consequences of a bite by a dog that had never known anything but his own family, within his own four walls. I never thought about the needs dogs have for an enriched living environment and the mental stimulation that comes from experiencing the world in all its novelty.

5. A dog that shows aggression must be immediately and severely punished.

When my 4-month-old German Shepherd lunged at a larger dog in obedience class, during the standard block heeling exercise with which we started each class meeting, the instructor screamed at her. I was told to do an Alpha Roll immediately, to "let her know who's boss," and that evening Honey exchanged her buckle for a prong collar.

I did everything wrong with Honey. Instead of managing her unwanted behavior and training alternative behaviors that were acceptable, I simply avoided taking her anywhere. Not knowing that there were trainers and behaviorists who could help me, I tried to "protect" her from the real world for her whole life. We took our walks only late at night, when no one else was likely to be out with their dogs. We hiked only in the most remote areas. If I did happen to see another dog (and I was so watchful, wherever we went), I tensed and tightened my grip on the leash, giving her solid support for her fearful aggression. It was only during the final two years of her life that I learned about desensitization and positive reinforcement and began to "train" friends who visited to give her treats.

6. Don't start training a dog until it's at least 6 months old.

"Let it be a dog!" they used to say. "Being a dog" apparently meant being wild, undisciplined, and out of control. It meant nipping the heels of children, stealing the Thanksgiving turkey off the kitchen counter, destroying the owner's possessions, digging up the flower beds, chasing the cat, barking at passersby, jumping on visitors and mounting their legs, and eating the kitty litter. "Training" apparently meant something awful, cruel, painful, repressive, and spirit-breaking. And there was some truth in that description. In the Dark Ages, most training methods were too harsh for anything but a hard, touch-insensitive police-dog-in-training—not the methods to which you'd want to subject your pet.

This image of training comes out of our culture's ideas about education in general. We think of school as "work" and recess as "play". After we graduate, we carry that same image with us into adulthood where we make a sharp distinction between work and play, between office and home, between public (where restraints are in force) and private (where we can relax and be ourselves).

When I started clicker training Ruby, my first all-clicker puppy, when she was seven weeks old, I was amazed at her insatiability for learning. She never wanted to stop working. Then, a friend suggested that maybe Ruby didn't think of training as work but as play. By the time she was 6 months old, she not only knew all the Novice and some of the advanced competition obedience exercises but, much more important, she knew how to learn.

7. Once you've taught a dog to heel on leash, off-leash heeling comes naturally.

I had taken Lily through several obedience classes, and my instructors were encouraging me to show her at the local obedience trial. No one ever told me that you had to teach a dog to heel off leash as well as on. My instructors were exhibitors themselves, and maybe they thought this was too obvious to have to tell their students.

On the day of the trial, I was most worried about her Recall, but that was beautiful. What wasn't beautiful was her off-leash heeling. She lagged so far behind me, with her ears flat against her head and her tail between her legs, that the judge asked me if I beat her. Was he serious or joking? I have no idea. I was so mortified that I just wanted to get out of that ring as quickly as possible. It was several years before I even thought about showing a dog again.

Ironically, I now do all my early training off leash, and I do everything I can to keep the leash out of the hands of my students. I now believe that, once you've trained a dog to heel off leash, working on leash is much easier. After all, it isn't the leash that teaches a dog to heel. On the contrary, a leash in the hands of an inexperienced or inept trainer is a hindrance.

8. If you just give the right command, the dog will do what you ask.

I still have students who ask me what command to use for such-and- such behavior—as if dogs knew English! I now know that most dogs respond much better to visual than to verbal cues. I also appreciate how context-dependent dogs are. A friend of mine was in the Novice ring, and the judge instructed her to "finish"—to swing into Heel position on her left side. In the stress of the moment, my friend forgot herself. Instead of giving her usual "Swing" command to her dog, she said "Finish." And the dog went smartly to Heel position! My friend still blushes at the memory, but 1 find it not at all surprising. After all, every good Novice-trained dog knows that that what we do after coming to Front is move into Heel position. My husband tells me that I'm going about this dog-training business backwards. Why not just teach the dogs English first, and then tell them what you want them to do!

9. Dogs work in order to please their owners.

That's why we didn't use food in training in the Dark Ages. We didn't want our dogs to "work for the food." When my students ask me about this, I ask them if they'd stay at their jobs for only pats on the back and no paychecks. I used to give my dogs treats only at bedtime—and for doing nothing. I thought this was an expression of my love for them. I wanted to believe that they were expressing their love for me by performing without the payoffs that really counted for them. Nowadays, 1 view training less as a mutual love fest and more as a dialogue, a form of communication, in which each of us gets satisfaction—though the satisfaction may differ in form. (I much prefer white chocolate macadamia nut cookies to freeze-dried liver.)

10. If you give your dog "people food," it will never again be satisfied with dog food.

Here's another culture-bound distinction we used to make that enabled us to differentiate between "people" and "animals" (as if people were not animals). Most people forget that, before there was "dog food," people fed their dogs a portion of their own meals. This is still true in parts of Europe, even among "civilized" and well-educated pet owners. I suspect that what we really meant to say was: don't feed your dog when he begs at the dinner table.

In our training, back in the Dark Ages, we not only refrained from giving our dogs food, but, if we ever did dispense treats, they were always large, hard, and crunchy—guaranteed to interrupt the flow of learning. And the treats were given well after the behavior we were working on was completed and when the dog was doing something entirely different. If you give a dog a treat while she is leaping in the air out of a Sit, she will not understand that it's the Sit you are rewarding.

But even in my Dark Ages days of ignorance, I did learn something that I don't ever want to forget: that I love my dogs with a passion, regardless of flaws, faults, or diseases. When I anthropomorphized my dogs as being "stubborn," "ornery," or "deceitful," I was really talking about myself as an inept trainer. I know that my students feel the same love for their dogs. My job is to guide them towards a better understanding of who their dogs really are.

To me, the most touching moment in a beginners' class is the first minute of the first night with dogs. I watch each owner (or couple or family) come in, a little hesitantly, with their dog. Both dog and human pause at the threshold and look around the room warily. Who are these other dogs (people)? Will 1 like them? Will they like me? The love that people feel for their dogs is so wondrous that it's often enough to see them through major behavior, training, and medical problems. It's this love that motivates me to want to help in any way I can. And, remembering my own Dark Ages, I can be more empathetic.

CHAPTER 3
Three Ways to Reach a "Difficult" Student

"Keep your left hand at your waist," I called out to Hilary who was teaching her dog focused heeling by feeding him with her left hand. Then I realized that this had been my constant refrain to her for these past 3 weeks of the beginners' class. Before I knew it, my Great Teacher instinct moved me to action. I walked up behind Hilary, gently held her left wrist to her waist, and instructed her to keep moving with her dog. She took two steps and then stopped abruptly. "Oh! So that's what you meant."

Hilary is one of the great majority of Americans who do not use sound to process information. Instead, she learns best through touch. A relatively new field of psychology, called Neuro-Linguistic Programming (NLP for short), studies what they call "modalities" of communication: sight (Visual), sound (Auditory), and touch/taste/smell/emotion (Kinesthetic). Each of us has our characteristic, preferred, and most practiced ways of processing information from the world around us.

Most Americans are primarily visual—hence, the richness of visual language, metaphors, and images we use: "Do you see what I mean?" "It's all clear to me now." Even the ultimate test of truth: "Seeing is believing!" Many of us are primarily kinesthetic, like Hilary, learning through the senses of touch, taste, smell, and

37

emotion. If your primary modality is kinesthetic, for example, you're likely to remember a dog show by the crush of the crowd, the smell of liver, the cold sweat in your palms, the feeling of excitement.

A small minority of Americans learn best through their auditory channel. What registers with them and remains in their memory is sound: the sound of the instructor's voice, the vocalizations of a Siberian husky in class, the tapping of canine feet on the training floor.

This model of learning styles helps us deal with the occasional "difficult" student. Maybe the source of the difficulty is that she and I process information through different modalities. Instead of *talking* to Hilary, all I had to do was *touch* her and put her arm in the correct position—communicating in her preferred kinesthetic modality.

Another "difficult" student, Jerome, never seemed to be watching me as I demonstrated how to teach the about turn and never got it right. After class, when I talked him through the process, he suddenly understood—clearly, an auditory person.

Betty, on the other hand, turned out to be a visual learner. I made use of this by drawing chalk marks on the floor to teach her better handling in the Figure Eight.

Now, here's the tricky part about these NLP modalities. The same event can be processed in any of the three modalities. For example, I'm a primarily visual processor. When I listen to music, I actually see it in my mind's eye—not the notes on the page of the musical score but something that's more like an architectural drawing, consisting of columns, aisles, rooms, doorways, and staircases. Yet, it would seem that listening to music would elicit an auditory thought process. Not for me!

It is also true that my processing preference has nothing to do with my competence or talent in that area. So, for example, though I am strongly visual in how I take in, store, and retrieve information, I'm useless when it comes to drawing. I can't seem to see the basket of fruit that is my subject in a way that would enable me to draw it. I see it as a whole—a basket of fruit—and I have to be taught to see it as a composition of shapes and different light values.

The point is that we can't usually guess at a student's learning-style preference. We can, however, watch, listen, and experiment in order to determine what it is. A student who has that famous glazed look of non-comprehension might simply be struggling to translate what I'm doing or saying into a form that she can make sense of. A student who seems bored with the class and is looking at the floor when I talk might be processing everything fully—but in his own auditory way.

How to find out what's really going on? Simple! I can ask—but in a very specific way. I can frame my questions so as to reach students with any of the three learning-style preferences. I like to start teaching a new behavior by demonstrating with one of the class dogs. Afterward, I might ask, in quick succession: "Is that clear? (visual) How does that sound to you? (auditory) Do you have a feeling about how this might work?" (kinesthetic) These are all very open-ended, nonspecific questions, designed to reach the visual, the auditory, and the kinesthetic learner.

What about homework? How can we design it so that every student will read it and follow the instructions? Well, to be perfectly frank, we can't. Homework is usually distributed as writing on a piece of paper—a pretty static, one-dimensional format. But there are things we can do that might get past this. We might, for example, hand out the homework and briefly "clarify" it by talking it through with the class.

I've also succeeded in reaching students who don't learn best by reading by including some auditory or kinesthetic instructions in the homework. For example, I instruct them to count out the duration of a Stay by saying "one ba-na-na" as the equivalent of one second. Somehow, these bananas of mine are more appealing and attention-getting than simply counting "seconds"—especially to the auditory and kinesthetic students. Banana counting also has the advantage that you can count fractions of a second by uttering only part of the phrase—so, for example, "one ba" is half a second. My students love that! And my kinesthetic students have always enjoyed the "fridge grid" I hand out—a sheet of paper they can attach to their fridge door with a magnet that lays out a matrix in which they can record, for each day, which of the homework behaviors they've worked on.

Once we understand these basic differences in communication and learning style, we are no longer tempted to judge and even dismiss our students as being stupid or uncooperative. In fact, maybe there's really no such thing as a "difficult" student. Or, maybe more accurately, my "difficult" student will be different from yours, simply because of our own learning-style preferences. In a sense, we might simply be speaking different languages— and "different" is often translated as "difficult."

How about, instead, if we delight in our differences and stretch ourselves by trying to close the gaps between us. Then, we can honestly say to our students: I see you, I hear you, I empathize with you.

CHAPTER 4
Guiding Students Towards New Beliefs About Their Dogs

"You can't learn anything without giving something up."

—Ramson Lomatewama, Hopi educator

What do the following statements have in common?

"She doesn't like to sit."

"I thought he was scared when he whined, so I petted and reassured him."

"My older dog was sad and feeling abandoned when I brought the new puppy home."

"He knew he'd been bad."

"The dogs we had when I was a kid never did that."

Yes, most of these are anthropomorphic statements, attributing human emotions to dogs. But more important, all these statements represent ideas, theories, or beliefs about dogs—what they are, how they should be. Our students come to us not only for something but with something. They bring lots of baggage from their past experience: vague ideas, untested theories, and beliefs that have the intensity of tenets of faith. The ideas don't usually get in the way of learning, and the sacred beliefs are often too tightly held for us to shake. The theories, on the other hand, are the real trouble-makers! Unquestioned, they begin to resemble Truth, and people act as if they were indeed true.

41

Let's look at the theories behind the statements quoted above and the actions those theories lead to.

"She doesn't like to sit."

Theory: Dogs have conscious preferences.

Action: I'll respect her preference and not persist in teaching her to sit.

"I thought he was scared when he whined, so I petted and reassured him."

Theory: Dogs feel emotions and express them vocally.

Action: Every time he whines, I'll pet him and tell him it's okay.

"My older dog was sad and feeling abandoned when I brought the new puppy home."

Theory: Dogs feel emotions that I can identify because they're the same emotions I would feel in a given situation.

Action: I'll reassure my dog with words and petting when she feels abandoned.

"He knew he'd been bad."

Theory: Dogs know right from wrong and act guilty and remorseful when they've done wrong.

Action: When he acts guilty, I'll punish him.

"The dogs we had when I was a kid never did that."

Theory: All dogs are the same—just like the ones I remember from my childhood.

Action: I decide that this dog is (stupid, vicious, wimpy, hard-headed...) and treat her accordingly.

To summarize these theories: Dogs are sentient, reasoning beings with conscious preferences, emotions, and a sense of morality. (Sounds a lot like people, doesn't it!) Dogs are like children and must be raised correctly.

Not surprisingly, the actions that follow from these theories reflect our culture's theories about parenting. For example, just as we punish children who have reached a certain age, assuming that their misbehavior is deliberate, so too we come down hard on dogs who "should know better."

If we didn't simplify experience by creating theories, we'd be overloaded with information. As instructors, we, too, have our theories about canine behavior and learning. The big difference between us and our students is that we're constantly testing our theories and, if necessary, changing them to fit observed reality. For example, we've learned that positive reinforcement of a behavior will strengthen that behavior. Consequently, we refrain from petting a whining dog who is complaining that his dinner is late! We also know that a dog's "preferences" are based mostly on which behaviors we've reinforced. As a result, we work hard at training dogs to "want" to do what we ask of them.

The better we understand that people act on their theories, right or wrong, the more effective we can be as instructors. For example, when I see a student lean menacingly over her dog and, in a threatening voice, say "Dammit, sit!" I remind myself that she believes she's doing the right thing. My job, as her instructor, is to challenge her theories about dog behavior. Only by making the student aware of her theories and offering alternatives do I have a chance of helping her change her dog's behavior.

If I'd had any doubt about the truth of this statement, it was completely dispelled when I met Sylvia and her dog Gypsy. "I can't believe this is my dog." Sylvia repeated this statement at least 10 times during the hour we spent together at my training facility. As we talked, Gypsy, a silky-coated, chocolate-brown, soulful-eyed Lab mix, lay quietly at Sylvia's feet.

Before we met for this private session, Sylvia and I had talked on the phone. She had described Gypsy as hyperactive, in constant motion, chasing the kids in the yard, and peeing on the carpet whenever she managed to slip into the house and was noisily chased out again. Hearing this description, I had prepared for our visit by asking my veterinarian if he'd be interested in co-consulting on the case, lending his pharmacological skills to my behavioral training. But the instant I met Gypsy in person, it was quite clear that there was absolutely nothing wrong with her—except for her owner's perception.

Sylvia had brought with her not only Gypsy but also a whole steamer trunk full of ideas, beliefs, and theories about dogs. Unconscious and unquestioned, these theories had the power of Truth and guided Sylvia's behavior with Gypsy. The specific theory that had brought us together was that a "good" dog was quiet and calm, naturally compliant, and willing to live her life outdoors with only intermittent human company. No doubt, this theory was based on Sylvia's childhood experience with dogs. She talked lovingly of her family's dogs—how smart and well-behaved they were, how they would walk her to the school bus and be there to greet her when she returned home. Who fed the dogs? Who took them to the vet for their shots? Well, Sylvia thought, it must have been Mom who was home all day. Who bathed them when they got skunked? Who cleaned up puppy accidents in the kitchen? Oh, Sylvia said, they were never allowed in the house.

And so Sylvia, like many others, grew up with a theory about dogs and how to keep them. Dogs were angelic beings, loving and protective by nature, good to have around when there were kids in the family—but, unfortunately, not very clean. When Sylvia had her own children, she dutifully provided them with a dog and perpetuated her youthful canine fantasies in the minds of her offspring. Being the Mom, however, she was now the one "home all day" to deal with Gypsy. She concluded that there must be something wrong with this dog, so unlike the dogs of her childhood.

My task, as behavior consultant, was to challenge Sylvia's theories and help her create new ones that might be more useful. Gypsy herself made this easy. Even though this was probably her first trip away from home, except for visits to the vet, she remained calm and self-assured—not at all the "hyperactive" banshee that Sylvia had described. Sylvia's repeated statement, "I can't believe this is my dog," expressed her amazement and confusion. Certainly, this dog was Gypsy—and yet, she was not the Gypsy that Sylvia knew. Sylvia was in chaos, not knowing what to believe.

If we had done nothing but sit and talk for an hour, Sylvia might have been able to resolve the conflict between her old theories and the evidence before her eyes in a superficial way. She might have, for example, decided that Gypsy was "behaving" only because of being in a new place—just as children are often said to behave better away from home. But then I went on to show Sylvia how to teach Gypsy to sit, lie down, and walk nicely at her side. The dog was bright, willing, and responsive. Sylvia's earlier tension and confusion gave way to smiles and laughter as she tried all of this.

Only when she seemed to accept this new "truth"—that her dog was actually quite nice and very educable—could we spend some time talking about the home situation and how to solve some of the problems the family was having with Gypsy. By the time Sylvia and Gypsy left, I felt certain that things would be different, because Sylvia had started building a new theory about dogs in general and this one in particular.

The story of Sylvia and Gypsy exemplifies a powerful model of how we learn. Jean Piaget, a Swiss psychologist, contested earlier theories of learning that described people as "blank slates" or "empty vessels." Depending on the metaphor, learning was either "written" on our minds or "poured" into us like Gatorade. We were simply passive receptacles. Piaget discovered that real learning requires that the learner engage with—even struggle with—the environment. Here's how the process works.

We start with our old theories about the world, based on past experience—for example, Sylvia's childhood fantasies about dogs that led her to think there was something wrong with Gypsy. We encounter something that challenges these theories, creating a momentary chaos in our minds—"I can't believe this is my dog." In order to resolve the contradiction and relieve our chaos, we must take some kind of action. We swing back and forth between denying the new evidence so that we can hold on to our old theories or deciding to dump those theories in favor of the new "truth." We keep swinging, pendulum-like, until we come to rest in a new place of balance that makes sense and feels right. Yes, there is some truth in the old theories. And yes, the new evidence does put them in a different light. When we reach this new place, Piaget said, we have created new knowledge for ourselves.

Think about the many ways you use this model of learning in your classes. For example, if you ask people not to bring their dogs to the first class meeting, you are challenging their theory that dog school is only about training dogs! When you seat people and their dogs at widely spaced intervals, you are challenging anthropomorphic theories people hold about their dog's need to "socialize" with other dogs. Humor, too, is a great way to challenge old theories. For example, when a student says to his dog "Sit, sit, sit," you ask him how many dogs he's training. In the delicious moment of chaos that follows, the student creates an important new learning for himself, much more effectively than you could have done by admonishing him not to repeat a command.

I believe that our task as instructors is to guide our students through this process. First, we offer challenges to their theories, throwing them into chaos. Then we support our students with information and reassurance as they struggle with the contradictions. And finally, we celebrate them when they arrive at their own new learning.

Recommended Reading

Piaget, Jean

The volume and range of Piaget's work is enormous. A good place to start learning about his life and work is at the website of the Jean Piaget Society: <http://www.piaget.org>

CHAPTER 5
What Happens When We Treat Dogs As If They're People

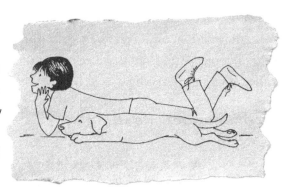

"*Well, Dani, I did what you said. When Greta didn't come when I called, I casually strolled over to a bench and started humming. And then she just went crazy!*"

I pondered this for a moment, trying to understand what my student Don was saying. Images of Greta, the Bernese Mountain Dog, falling into a seizure leaped through my mind. Or starting to dance a fantastic jig. Or throwing herself on the ground in a wild tantrum.

"*What do you mean—'crazy'?*" I asked Don. "*What did Greta do?*"

"*Well, she just went crazy.*"

Even when we're talking about our fellow humans, this is hardly a descriptive word. But when we're talking about dogs, what I hear is an extreme case of anthropomorphizing—attributing to dogs the thoughts, emotions, and associated behaviors of human beings.

My dictionary tells me that "crazy" means either: *Being afflicted by or manifesting unsoundness of mind or an inability to control one's rational processes.*—**or**—*Felt to be ridiculous because not exhibiting good or conventional sense.*

48

Either way, we're making some pretty big assumptions about dogs! And that's probably why anthropomorphism is a taboo—like "instinct" in psychology and "human nature" in anthropology. A lot has been written about the evils of anthropomorphizing our dogs. Vicki Hearne, in her book *Adam's Task,* talks about the "humaniacs" and how they reduce the dignity of the dog by transforming it into a quasi-human. Surprisingly, Hearne admires Elizabeth Marshall Thomas who, in her book *The Hidden Life of Dogs,* makes no secret of her wish to "understand" dogs by anthropomorphizing them. Then there's William Campbell, a highly respected canine behaviorist whose *Behavior Problems in Dogs* has had a major influence on dog training. He firmly believes that dogs both think and feel. And a book by Masson and McCarthy, *When Elephants Weep,* makes a strong argument for the reality of emotions in non-human animals.

I'm not particularly interested in the question of whether or not dogs feel emotion, and I'm certainly not interested in taking sides on the anthropomorphism issue. What I am interested in is what this way of thinking does to us and to our students.

I see two kinds of effects that come from anthropomorphizing dogs. One of them is connection. When we anthropomorphize dogs, we increase our connectedness, and we build stronger bonds across our two species. Since we have only ourselves to use as a baseline for understanding the world and the other animals in it, in a sense the highest compliment we can pay to another creature is to say: you are like me. When we anthropomorphise in this way, we can actually increase our understanding of dogs— maybe not on a logical or rational level, but on a supra-logical level. We become more aware of our connection with all other species on this earth. We open ourselves to the joy and love that comes from living with dogs.

For example, I recognize that my dog and I share very similar reactions to stressors. Although we are not physiologically identical, our hormonal responses are enough alike to lead both of us into a state of negative stress, in which we simply shut down. When that happens—to either of us—I conclude wisely that this is not a good time to train.

I also believe my veterinarian who tells me that his clients often know more about their dogs than he does. They can sometimes detect a pathological state sooner than any laboratory test or physical examination. People are simply more attuned to the slightest behavioral changes in their dogs, without even being able to articulate what those are. In these cases, anthropomorphism becomes a form of empathy, leading to deeper understanding and knowledge.

The other side of anthropomorphism is, to me, about closing doors. When we use anthropomorphism to explain canine behavior, we're saying: "Oh, that's nothing but...(happiness, jealousy, sulking, whatever you like)." In other words, we observe behavior and arrive at conclusions about its meaning based on what that behavior might mean if it came from a person.

Whenever we use a theory or a model to explain behavior, we are bound to close some doors. That, after all, is the great value of models: they simplify a complex world. We say, "Let's pretend that this model is true, and let's explore the implications." The trouble with the anthropomorphism model is not the model itself but what we do with it. We're not using it as a "Let's pretend" or a "What if" model that might clarify and illuminate. We're using it, instead, to discount the dog's behavior.

For example, Louise comes home and finds a mess on the carpet, starts screaming at her dog, Homer, sees him cower and finally slink away, and says "He knows he did wrong." But do we really know that? Dog trainers and behaviorists tell us that dogs live in the moment, in the here-and-now. And isn't that one of the characteristics that so endears them to us? But if Homer is indeed living in the moment, that means that he must have just now created the mess on the carpet, seconds before Louise arrives. What if he didn't? What if this happened an hour before Louise's arrival? There's no evidence that dogs "remember" and make connections like this over time.

There is, however, lots of evidence that dogs respond to the immediate words, postures, gestures, and facial expressions that we humans emit. Let's go back to Louise's arrival. She opens the front door, sees the mess on the carpet, utters a big sigh, maybe coupled with a few choice words that might include "Not again!" She drops her purse and coat on the floor, puts both hands on her hips, and glowers at her dog who has come to greet her. Homer takes this all in and—heads for the hills. What he "knows" is not that he did wrong but that Louise is very, very angry at him. Survival instincts are strong and healthy in most dogs, so we should not be surprised that Homer decides to leave the scene quickly.

Louise is not only dismissing what Homer is telling her in his own language. She's also justifying those actions of hers that will follow the event. Her rage and whatever actions it leads her to are validated by the assumption that her dog "knows better." In other words, Louise believes that her dog is like her. He has the ability to make moral decisions and to accept the consequences of his actions, even if the time interval between action and consequence is several hours.

When Louise buys into the belief that this model is a true one, not just a "Let's pretend," she has some choices. She can become blaming, angry, harsh, and punishing. She can inflict physical pain and, certainly, psychological pain on Homer. Or she can become over-solicitous and over-protective, soothing and reassuring Homer and thereby reinforcing his submissive behavior. Based as they are in anthropomorphism, however, none of Louise's behavior choices will help her solve the problem that generated them—the mess on the carpet.

So how does Louise solve the problem, now that she's taking a fresh, more objective view of it? Probably the simplest solution is a two-parter. In Part One, Louise says Hello to Homer, ushers him kindly into another room, and cleans up the mess with something that will also remove the odor (like an enzyme-based cleaner) so that Homer won't be tempted to use the same spot again.

In Part Two, Louise tries to determine the source of the problem. If this is a rare event, then maybe Homer is suffering from a digestive upset or a urinary-tract infection—in which case, it's not really his fault that he couldn't control himself. If, on the other hand, this is a regular event in Louise and Homer's life, she will have to think about ways to end the pattern, maybe by installing a dog door, or limiting Homer's access to carpeted areas of the house, or maybe even by reeducating him about desirable toilet etiquette (that is, redoing his house-training).

Louise has now learned an important principle of dog training. Anthropomorphism, when it's used to explain behavior, usually leads us down dead-end roads. It leads us away from our problems and their possible solutions. It leads us away from thinking with an open mind, gathering information, withholding judgment, remaining objective—and, at the same time, caring.

Once my student Don realized that Greta was not "crazy," he was forced to find other, more accurate, explanations of her refusal to come when called. In that moment, he opened himself to new possibilities and went into a genuine problem-solving frame of mind. What it took to help him get there was my gentle but firm insistence that he describe Greta's behavior.

"Yes," I acknowledged, *"she 'went crazy.' And what did she do next?"*

"She came over to the bench I was sitting on, desperate for attention."

I tactfully ignored this second "explanatory" anthropomorphism and asked again:

"And what did she do then?"

"She just stood still and looked at me."

"What did you do?"

"Well, I remembered what you had told us in class, so I praised her."

Don had just demonstrated the first lesson in getting a dog to come when called: Always make it a positive experience, even if the Recall is not entirely up to your standards. There's plenty of time to work on that part of the problem later, after you've persuaded your dog that it's worthwhile to come at all. Don had also passed a huge milestone in his progress towards becoming a good dog trainer. He now understood that it was useless to make anthropomorphic assumptions about Greta's behavior. Maybe even worse than useless, since those assumptions seemed to lead only to frustration for Don. Instead, both he and Louise were able to solve their problems by temporarily disengaging emotionally from their dogs and becoming clear-thinking observers of the behaviors before them. To put it another way, they were able to ask themselves if this was a situation in which anthropomorphism would lead to heightened connection with their dogs or to a dismal failure in solving a problem.

Recommended Reading

Milani, Myma M., D.V.M.

1986   The Body Language and Emotion of Dogs.

Milani explains the fundamentals of dog behavior and shows us how to use this knowledge in training. The book is especially good at helping us understand that dogs are not just little people but a different species.

CHAPTER 6
On the Road to Smooth Communication

You're on your way home after the third meeting of your beginners' class. Your mind keeps returning to an interaction you had with a student. You find yourself going over and over what she said and what you said and what she said and what

you said.... And suddenly you realize that you're going around in circles trying to figure out what went wrong with the conversation. You're not even sure that anything went wrong, but you are left with an uncomfortable feeling about the whole event. The content of the conversation has grown fuzzy in your mind, and all that remains is the bad feeling. Congratulations! You've just reinvented the Communication Wheel.

Imagine the wheel of an old-fashioned, horse-drawn cart. The wheel is composed of three pie-shaped sections—Self, Other, and Context. We can describe any interaction between people in terms of these three elements. In a good communication, we pay attention to all three elements and the wheel turns smoothly. When we fail to honor one or more of these, the wheel collapses in those sections and communication stumbles along or even groans to a halt. "That's it!" you say, "That's exactly how it felt as the conversation went on."

The Communication Wheel

Let's look at some of the possibilities when we fail to pay attention to a section of the Communication Wheel. For example, have you ever accepted a student whom you felt you could not refuse, even though his dog was too hyper-reactive to other dogs to be ready for a class experience? Maybe this person was a club member with six Obedience-Trial-Champion dogs, and you felt a little intimidated. Or maybe he was a struggling graduate student who could not afford private lessons. Whatever the case, if you were discounting your own beliefs and needs to accommodate his, you were deflating the Self section of the Communication Wheel, and your communication was doomed to falter and, finally, fail.

I came very close to upsetting the balance of the Communication Wheel in a recent class when I felt my anger coming up about a student who had missed several classes and had not been working with her dog between classes. When I called her on the morning of our next class to remind her that we were meeting in a different place that evening, she said: "Oh, I was going to call you. I won't be in class tonight because it's my son's birthday and he wants to go to a movie." My frustration nearly got the best of me, and I was on the verge of venting it on her—paying no attention to the Other section of the wheel. But then I reminded myself that her transparent avoidance of coming to class was not surprising, considering how little success she was having with her difficult dog. The combination of her class absences and her failure to train during the week had gradually depleted her self-confidence. If anything, it was my fault for not having noticed and corrected the situation earlier.

I am aware of Context when I teach my Pet Partners class, for people who are working towards certifying their dogs to do Animal Assisted Activities or Therapy. I spend a lot of time discussing canine behavior. We consider how to recognize and manage stress in a dog, how to identify each dog's unique configuration of drives, and how to use calming signals to communicate with our dogs. All of these are important subjects for people who will be doing the demanding and difficult work of visiting healthcare facilities with their dogs. But if I introduced these subjects in my general-public beginners' class, I would lose my audience in no time. In that very different context, I need to stick to the basic, practical, and concrete issues, lest I disturb the balance of the Communication Wheel.

Paying attention to the Self section of the wheel means that I honor my own needs when I am stressed or fatigued—perhaps by taking a short break in the middle of a class. It means, too, that I know myself and what kinds of things are difficult or unpleasant for me. For example, I always experience some anxiety as I prepare for the first meeting of a new class. Until I have actually met my students and their dogs, I worry about who they are, what they want, if they'll enjoy the class, how quickly the dogs will learn, and on and on. Instead of ignoring or making light of these concerns, unproductive as they might be, I face them directly. Taking care of Self, in this case, usually spills over into taking care of Other, for I realize that my students are also uneasy and apprehensive about this first class meeting.

For instructors, the Other section of the Communication Wheel includes our students, colleagues, assistants, and even the dogs. What about the just-adopted shelter dog who disrupts the entire class by barking nonstop? What about the 8-year-old student who weighs less than her Great Dane? What about the student with Cerebral Palsy who adores her bouncing Beardie? What about the man who is bringing "his wife's" dog to class because she's out of town? What about the student who has written books on dog training and is coming to class "just to socialize" her dog? What about the student who is in class as a condition of her probation after being found guilty of keeping "too many" dogs?

I've had every single one of these Others in my classes, and I've often been tempted to discount them because of my own feelings of irritation, frustration, anger, amusement, inadequacy, contempt, or just plain uncertainty about how to deal with the situation. Paying attention to the Other section of the Communication Wheel means noticing, acknowledging, and respecting where the Other is coming from. One of my sweetest teaching experiences was getting acquainted with the court-referred student who started the class sullen and unreceptive and ended as a devoted student and good friend. As the Other, she felt accepted and unpressured, and that allowed her the space she needed to make her own choice about training, rather than simply being coerced by the court.

Paying attention to Context on the Communication Wheel means that we are aware of the environmental, temporal, spatial, and geographic circumstances of a class. One of the first classes I ever taught was in a city park, next to a major highway and complete with mosquitoes, high winds (though not strong enough to blow the mosquitoes away), kids playing softball, teenagers with boomboxes, and dogs running loose all around us. For about 15 minutes, I shouted at my students, keeping an eye out for stray balls and dogs that slipped their collars and were heading for the highway. Finally, I paid attention to Context by cancelling the class until we could find a different location.

The following week, we moved to the second-floor lounge of an office building. The floor was carpeted, the furniture new and clean, and there were floor-to-ceiling glass partitions around our "classroom." Even though the dogs had to go up a long, narrow, steep flight of stairs to get there, this was an improvement!

I have also taught in church buildings with floors so heavily waxed that a dog trying to Sit would slide immediately into a Down. To make it even more interesting, our class met on the same evening as choir practice, and I must admit that the music was soothing.

Other Context factors include class size, composition, level of experience, and cost. Our local obedience club learned the hard way about paying attention to Context when they offered a free beginners' class to anyone who adopted a dog from our city's shelter. Very soon, it became clear that this generous offer was doomed to fail—all because of lack of attention to Context. Many of the students, though well-intentioned, seemed to know nothing about dogs. Some of them never even showed up for the first class because they had already returned their dogs to the shelter. Those who did come to class, struggling with all the issues they were facing as adopters, sometimes got little more than the standard "How to Teach Your Dog to Sit" instead of the help they desperately needed with behavior problems.

One of my favorite examples of paying attention to Context comes from my own experience as an advanced competition-obedience student. Every year, right around Thanksgiving week, the teacher announced to our class that, with the holidays coming and taking up so much of our time and attention, we would not start on anything new. Instead, we'd play games and have fun, as befits the season! In spite of the heightened demands of that time of year, our class attendance never dropped off.

Recognizing Incongruence

It's not always easy to keep the Communication Wheel rolling smoothly. Sure, there are rocks and ruts out there on the road that must be negotiated, but the biggest influence on communication usually comes from inside—from the hub of the wheel, to continue the analogy. When my self-worth is high, when I'm rested and healthy, when I'm feeling confident and strong, the wheel turns smoothly and easily as I honor the needs of each of the three components. Virginia Satir taught us how to improve communication through Congruence—what I express outwardly fits with what I'm feeling inside.

If I'm tired or sad or worried, I need to acknowledge that at least to myself and maybe to my students, rather than pretending that it's "business as usual." If I'm frustrated with a student who isn't training at home, I might tell her how I feel (privately, of course) rather than trying to hide my feelings under a thin veil of sarcasm in class. If my own dog is seriously ill, I let my students know why I'm a little teary, instead of denying my worry by delivering an impersonal lecture on the Second Fear Imprint Period. When I have stage fright during an important presentation to my colleagues, I let them in on it and allow them to see me as human, instead of discounting my feelings through silly and inappropriate joking.

But when the cartload of stress becomes too heavy, my self-worth may drop. Then I make the mistake of channeling much of my energy into protecting myself from imagined dangers and from my own painful feelings. Instead of maintaining the nice, easy balance of the Communication Wheel,

I unwittingly withdraw my attention from one or more parts of it. Instead of acknowledging and maybe even expressing my vulnerability, I go into a mindless state and behave in ways that are out of my control and awareness. Satir called these out-of-balance states Coping Strategies: Blaming, Placating, SuperReasonable, and Irrelevant.

The following examples of these incongruent coping strategies are drawn from a workshop on Communication that I taught for instructors of obedience classes. Most of them were skilled dog trainers and experienced obedience instructors. I had asked them to describe their biggest problem as obedience instructors. Their own words reveal clearly which of the coping strategies are their "favorites" for dealing with stress.

Noel: *"I feel that sometimes my instructions might not be clear enough. I also can be drawn into giving one person too much attention and I may not be firm enough."*

Noel discounts Self when he's under stress, using the incongruent coping strategy of Placating. His words are tentative and his manner uncertain. He finds fault only and always with himself. Satir taught us about placating by creating a concrete, exaggerated, physical picture. She would invite someone to role-play the placating person as a supplicant—down on his knees with one arm reaching out and the other pressed against his heart. The placator sees himself as wrong, and the Other in the communication as right. He discounts his own needs and submits to the Other's wishes and judgments.

Donald: *"I am unable to keep a smiling motivating face if I have one of those extra-stupid, extra-untalented classes."*

Donald deals with his stress by discounting Other on the communication wheel. He points a Blaming finger at his students. It's their fault. Of course, he doesn't make this statement directly to them but conveys his feelings in subtle, and not-so-subtle, ways by his words and tone of voice. He begins sentences with "You," putting the blame squarely on the Other. He uses a lot of "shoulds" in his instructions. He talks in absolutes about his students' efforts: "You always...," "You never...." He asks questions beginning with "Why (do/don't you)..." that can be answered only by an admission of guilt or ineptness. Not surprisingly, Donald reports, "My students are afraid of me."

Marsha: *"[My biggest problem is] dealing with the under-achiever or low-energy handler. I have a theory that achievers, or their achievements, are so admired by the less active that the goal changes from performing the feat to acquiring the trappings of those who perform the feat. During the initial telephone interview, I stress the amount of work to be done at home with the dog, point out the waste of time and money if the work is not done and the resultant embarrassment in class."*

Marsha deals with her stress by adopting the SuperReasonable coping strategy. She discounts both Self and Other—that is, the living, breathing human beings in the conversation—and pays attention only to the Context, the class requirements. She speaks in abstractions and uses the passive voice. She spins theories out of her head, anesthetizing all the emotional parts of her. She seeks refuge from her painful feelings by totally denying them and concentrating instead on "the facts."

Robert: *"When students ask me difficult questions about behavior, I just don't know where to begin. I shoot a volley of questions at them about the dog's health, living conditions, diet, exercise, place in the family... Before they have a chance to answer even the first question, I start telling them about hip dysplasia, barrier frustration, orthomolecular medicine, rage syndrome, acupuncture, and separation anxiety. Finally, I get **so** frustrated, I just want to walk away."*

Robert seeks relief from his stress through the incongruent coping strategy of Irrelevant behavior. He discounts all three parts of the Communication Wheel. He protects himself from perceived threat by distracting attention from himself, the student, and the classroom situation. As he himself realizes, his responses are not appropriate and do not address the student's question. These conversations often end with bewilderment on the part of the student and a feeling of helplessness in Robert.

Moving Towards Congruence

If you've recognized yourself in any of these instructors' statements, you have a high level of self-awareness and honesty. The fact is, all of us are capable of incongruence, because all of us are subject to dips and valleys in our self-esteem. Can we simply eradicate these incongruent coping strategies? Is there a pill, or a health farm, or a psychotherapist that can free us? No, and, if there were, we'd be in worse shape than we are in now. The coping strategies are hard-wired in us because they are, fundamentally, strategies for survival.

There are times when it's compassionate to be able to discount Self—for example, when a student's dog has been poisoned and she needs a shoulder to cry on. There are times when it's useful to discount Other—for example, when a dog fight erupts in class and you need to take action immediately, without considering how the owners of the fighters feel. There are times when it's rational to focus on Context only, to the exclusion of Self and Other—for example, when a tornado alert sounds and you must guide your students and their dogs quickly to the basement, ignoring their anxiety and your own fear. And there are times when discounting all the sections of the wheel helps to defuse a tense situation—for example, when the board of your obedience club is meeting with a member whose dog is dog-aggressive, and you suggest taking a short break so that the highly-charged emotions can cool.

These are all examples of how the incongruent coping strategies can serve as congruent and appropriate behavior. What makes them congruent in these cases? It's all about choice. Every one of these examples depends on a strong sense of self-worth, and each of these actions is chosen consciously, rather than "just happening." In a state of congruence, I am in charge of myself, my mind is functioning well, and I'm aware of what needs to be done. Because my self-worth is high at that moment, I can do what's necessary in a way that is most effective and least harmful.

But what if my behavior comes from low self-worth? What if I'm incongruent in my communication, sending messages that do not match my inner feelings? The simple secret is to set the Communication Wheel back in balance—simple, but not always easy! First, I must become of aware of my incongruent state. That's easy! Everyone has experienced one of those "bad-hair" days when everything seems to go wrong and you wish you had just stayed in bed. What you do with those feelings will move you into either incongruence or congruence.

I have a friend who is a social worker in a child-care agency. She introduced me to the idea of "mental health days"—those days when, if you did go to work, you'd probably spend the time in one or several of your favorite incongruent coping strategies— Blaming colleagues, Placating your boss, being SuperReasonable with clients, or hiding behind Irrelevance with everyone. Her agency, like many others in the mental health field, encourages staff to develop awareness of their emotional state and, if necessary, call in to say that they'll not be at work that day. As she explained to me, just the simple act of bringing to awareness your feeling of low self-worth is sometimes enough to turn it around. I've been able to do that, once the awareness is there, by simply taking a short walk, or throwing a ball for my dog, or just reminding myself to breathe!

Congruence does not mean always feeling good and acting happy. Quite the opposite. It does mean that, when I've been hit by one of life's nasty arrows and I'm feeling vulnerable, I can acknowledge that instead of allowing it to fester or be disguised. I can tell my assistant that I didn't find helpful something she did in class—instead of angrily Blaming her. I can end class early because I'm too tired to do a good job—instead of Placating the students and forcing myself to suffer through it to the bitter end. I can throw away the evening's lesson plan to concentrate on an exercise that everyone is having trouble with—instead of being SuperReasonable and falling back on what the class "should" know by this time. And I can even laugh at myself when I make a mistake in class—instead of being Irrelevant and trying to divert attention from what I've said or done.

In each of these cases, I am restoring the Communication Wheel to balance again by turning my attention to the element I've been discounting—Self, Other, Context, or a combination of these. This is possible only if I have first acknowledged my own feelings, and, interestingly, the very act of dealing with them congruently often restores my self-worth as well as improving communication.

Recommended Reading

Satir, Virginia
    1976   Making Contact.
    This small book is one of Satir's earliest. In it, she presents some of her major ideas. The book is a good, brief introduction to her work.

1988   The New Peoplemaking.

This is Satir's most popular and beloved book. In it, you'll find an expansion of her work on self-worth, communication, and change.

Weinberg, Dani

    1995   The Human-Canine Relationship: Lessons in Communication In: How To Be the Dog Trainer You Want To Be, Job Michael Evans

An earlier version of this chapter, written in 1992, in which the ideas are more fully elaborated. (Caution: It contains some notions about training dogs that I no longer hold!)

PART TWO: THE INSTRUCTOR

*"Every outstanding instructor
I know is also a lifelong student."*

Part Two—The Instructor

Now we're ready to talk about the other important human in the dog-training process, the instructor. Here's a summary of how we'll do this.

Chapter 7 asks the question: Who is responsible for learning— the trainer or the dog, the instructor or the student? Managing the environment is a way to bypass the learning process, whereas training (the dog) and teaching (the human student) can actually result in behavior change.

Chapter 8 shows how to enhance your teaching skill by recognizing your own ways of perceiving the world and making decisions, and then working with differences in how your students do this. The chapter describes several different problem-solving styles.

Chapter 9 highlights the importance of the physical characteristics of the training place and how they can add to or detract from students' learning and the instructor's satisfaction in teaching.

Once these issues of responsibility, problem-solving style, and the training place are resolved, we can look at teaching issues.

Chapter 10 is about how to mine the gold from the sometimes meager communication we get from students as "feedback."

Chapter 11 offers a set of "tools" for nurturing and preserving the essential foundation for effective instructing—the instructor's self-esteem.

Chapter 12 describes some specific areas for building self-esteem. Growing as an instructor requires that we appreciate qualities such as our personal characteristics, problem-solving ability, knowledge and continuing education, interpersonal skills, and sense of humor.

Chapter 13 offers ideas for dealing with the ultimate crisis of self-esteem—burnout.

Chapter 14 reminds us why we get paid for doing what we love. Once again, lowered self-esteem gets in the way, and we forget how valuable our work is to our students and their dogs.

Finally, Chapter 15 brings together many of the ideas in this book. It takes you with me as I walk in my students' mocassins. There's no better way to improve your instructing than to be a student yourself, and that's what I've done.

CHAPTER 7
When Management Ends and Learning Begins

"Training changes behavior, but management is forever—
a never-ending project."

When I first heard Shirley Chong, a gifted trainer and teacher, say these words at a seminar she was presenting, my mind screeched to a halt. For the next few minutes, I was so busy processing this seemingly radical idea that I didn't hear much else. Since that moment, I've given the idea lots of thought, observed it in practice, and experimented with it.

We all know that both training and management are legitimate strategies for influencing behavior. For example, we train our dogs to wait before jumping out of the car, but we also manage the situation by not opening the car door in heavy traffic—just in case. What interests me is how these strategies are different and how, by deepening our understanding of the differences, we can become better trainers and instructors. Management, to put it very simply, is what you do when training isn't feasible. Management is a way to influence behavior by reducing the dog's choices to only a single one—the "right" one We do this by manipulating the environment so that the undesired behavior cannot happen.

But are we sometimes too quick to reach for a management solution rather than considering a training possibility? And, in our haste to solve a problem, are we perhaps depriving the dog of an opportunity to change the behavior through learning?

To answer these important questions, we need to look more deeply at how the two strategies differ. When you manage, you're changing the dog's environment. When you train, you're changing the dog's behavior. When you manage, you're taking responsibility. When you train, you're giving the dog the opportunity to take responsibility for her behavior. When you manage, you're taking the active role in the process while the dog remains passive. When you train, you're inviting the dog to be active. And that's when learning happens.

I'm not saying that management is always the wrong strategy. I recognize that it's sometimes the only way to keep a dog safe—or even alive. I am saying, though, that we trainers and instructors too often leap directly and even mindlessly to management when there's a real possibility that the unwanted behavior can be changed through training.

When is management an appropriate choice?

An elderly and frail gentleman tries to walk an energetic, adolescent Labrador on leash, using a buckle collar—when a head halter might be an appropriate form of management. In this case, it's unlikely that the owner will be easily persuaded to train loose-leash walking.

A dog is known to be spooky around children—so he's crated at the Thanksgiving family gathering, with lots of children screaming and running around. In the unlikely event that this is the only day of the year that there might a problem, we can say that management is sometimes just a matter of short-term convenience. But this dog probably over-reacts to children on many other occasions that might lead to serious consequences. Management, then, is appropriate when we're concerned for the immediate safety of the dog and of others.

Management is also appropriate as an interim measure while training proceeds. When the dog's life or health are at stake, we can use management effectively while we allow the necessary training to take hold. But sometimes we're too quick to make a judgment that a situation is going to be harmful or dangerous to the dog or to others.

For example, my friend Tommy tells us about his Border Collie, Gambit, who is a "wild man" on the agility field:

"My management of Gambit when we're training agility is to keep him from losing control and going off to do agility on his own. I use a lot of voice to do this —a soft 'Good' when he's doing well and a loud 'Aargh' when he makes a mistake. I have learned to keep Gambit on a tight 'virtual' leash or he might go off and kill himself! The only punishment he gets is negative (denying him something he wants)—sometimes a short Down-Stay on the course, or time-outs in his crate for more serious infractions.

"Last night, I took Gambit to agility class. At first, he was a wild man, and I had to raise my volume and do some Down-Stays to get him under control. But I'm wondering if I am on the right track. It sounds like I'm managing Gambit in stressful situations instead of training him. While my methods seem to work in the short term, he does not seem to generalize and learn."

An even more subtle form of management occurs when we think we're actually training. I remember how I used to deal with my young German Shepherd, Ruby, who got very excited by the presence of other dogs at the park. Working close to the other dogs, I would put Ruby through her obedience paces—doing lots of Sits and Downs and short Recalls.

Was I teaching Ruby to learn how to cope with all the excitement around her, or was I simply distracting her from it? To answer that question, all we need to do is determine who was taking responsibility. Was it me, giving a steady stream of cues, or was it Ruby, voluntarily choosing to work? On the surface, it looked as if I was training Ruby, but, when we look more closely at the situation, we can see that I was really doing a very subtle kind of preventive management, very much like what Tommy was doing with Gambit. What was Ruby learning? Go ahead and do whatever you like, because your trainer will bring you back into focus!

Suzanne Hetts, an animal behaviorist, made a similar point in her presentation on aggression and phobias, "Implementing Counter Conditioning," at the Association of Pet Dog Trainers' annual conference in 1998. A common recommendation for handling aggressive behavior is to teach and then cue an incompatible behavior. For example, the dog is taught to respond to a Sit cue, instead of lunging and barking, when he sees another dog.

Hetts notes, however, that aggression is often fear-based, and the aggressive response has been learned through classical rather than operant conditioning—that is, by repeated association of the trigger (the other dog) and the fear response. We're dealing with a Conditioned Emotional Response. If we simply "counter-command" (by asking for an incompatible behavior) in the triggering situation, the dog will remain fearful, even though performing the cued behavior. We haven't changed the emotional response but only temporarily suppressed one expression of it. If, on the other hand, we "counter-condition"—that is, actually train a different emotional response, we will have changed the dog's behavior permanently, and the change will hold even in our absence.

A fearful-aggressive dog that sits at the handler's request when a trigger is present is being managed. The dog remains fearful and, if not for the presence of the handler, might easily go back to his previous behavior. But a dog that learns to remain calm, whether sitting or standing or lying down, in the presence of another dog, has been trained. The training process will include systematic desensitization and counter-conditioning, resulting in a different emotional and behavioral response. The dog has then gone beyond his trainer's control and moved towards self-control. In short, he is no longer being managed but has actually learned something new.

Management is a short-term tactic that often becomes a long-term (and tedious) "solution." If we start with management and fail to institute training, we will forever have to manage. Training, on the other hand, is a long-term solution that might start slowly and might be less effective in the early stages but ultimately will put the responsibility on the dog, take it off the owner, and provide a real solution for the long term.

Here are some classic examples of circumstances in which instructors typically recommend management—even though every one of these situations offers equally good, though maybe more difficult, possibilities for training.

1. Young puppies must be managed because they "don't know any better." We puppy-proof the house because puppies will "naturally" make the wrong choices. They're attracted to things that are dangerous to them, such as electric cords, garbage cans, and smelly slippers. We protect them from their own worst instincts by removing such objects from their reach. But, in addition to our (always imperfect!) attempts to puppy-proof the house, we can train the puppy to learn that certain objects (like electrical cords, slippers, garbage cans) smell or taste bad and, therefore, are best avoided.

74

2. Dogs must be managed because they're driven by genetically hardwired programs that compel them, for example, to chase anything that moves. So we build solid-wood fences as visual barriers on the street-facing side of the yard. Some dogs are driven to attack when they perceive a threat. So we outfit them in prong collars or head halters so that we can more easily turn them away from the object of their compulsion. Some dogs suffer from phobias. So we keep them indoors on the Fourth of July and send them outdoors when we vacuum the house.

But instead, we can train the prey-driven dog to make a different choice. We can train the fearful dog to learn that the presence of a stranger predicts a treat. We can train the phobic dog to decide that the vacuum cleaner produces nothing but white noise.

3. Dogs must be managed because we believe that they have no capacity for self-control. Without our interventions, they would revert back to the condition of their wild ancestors, and it would be impossible to live with them. In effect, we're saying that they're incapable of learning (even though life in the wild would be very short indeed if animals were truly incapable of learning).

While we cannot teach self-control directly, we can enable the dog to learn it by providing safe and reinforcing contexts. This approach might take a little more thought and planning than management strategies, but it's much more effective in the long run. And when we do it right, the lesson generalizes very quickly.

What better example of teaching a puppy self-control than housetraining! Of course, we must first establish a management foundation by confining the puppy when we're not present, watching her carefully when we are present, limiting water intake just before bedtime, thoroughly eliminating puppy-soiling odors, and putting meals, play sessions, and naps on a regular schedule so that we can anticipate when elimination might happen. But beyond that, there's really not much managing we can do. Puppies will be puppies and soil the house occasionally.

We can ignore "accidents," recognizing that that's all they are, and we can heavily reinforce successes. In short, we enable the puppy to teach herself some self-control over her own bodily functions. If we've done our job well, the puppy grows up with the ability to discriminate indoors from outdoors, in ways so subtle that we could probably not even begin to train the behavior. And we're so sure that the learning is complete that, later in the dog's life, we're likely to interpret lapses in housetraining as suggesting illness or other unusual causes.

Whether we're dealing with the dog's age or drives or degree of self-control, we can certainly take a moment to ask ourselves if it might be worth the extra thought and effort to educate rather than manage the dog's behavior. More often than not, the answer might be "Yes," and the effect might be more successful and long-lasting.

One of my favorite examples of the power of training over management comes from Leslie Lord, a trainer in Nova Scotia. "Blessed with lots of arrogant neighborhood animals who would prowl the fence line and tease the dogs," Leslie decided to train her 2-year-old Miniature Poodle, Simon, instead of following the traditional path of management. She writes:

"Can you see the grin on my face? Today, Simon chose to come to me rather than go after two squirrels that almost ran into him while he was doing a Sit-Stay."

Leslie describes how she accomplished this "miracle":

"Every time Simon blasted out of the house after yet another cat, I would calmly grab my clicker and treats and sit on the back step. I said nothing, never uttered a word to get his attention. As soon as Simon got tired of pounding on the fence and screaming at the long-gone cat and started back down the yard towards me, I would click and treat. Soon, I noticed that he spent almost no time barking and was quickly back to me, getting goodies. Soon, I couldn't even get out of the house and he was back. The day I saw him get halfway down the yard, stop, look back, and then tear back to me—that was the day I knew my plan was working."

One day, a perfect opportunity presented itself to test Simon's response to squirrels. Leslie and Simon were out walking.

"We paused to work on several informal recalls and a quick heel pattern. Then, I set him up for a formal recall and walked away. I was about to call him when the squirrels came into view. He jumped up—after all, the little boogers had almost crashed into him!—but hesitated for a nanosecond to look back at me. I smiled and calmly said 'Here'. He hesitated again and then came to me on the tear. Jackpot City! I gave him a jackpot of ten treats in a row, one after another. And then I released him. He looked back over his shoulder at where the squirrels had been, but I had already started to run up the path. He chose to follow me, and, as he reached me, it was jackpot time again. Did he have a choice? You bet! Did I assure him that he had made a really good choice? You bet!"

It's true that not all our students have the skill and patience that Leslie showed with Simon. It's also true that many students come to us when they're at their wit's end, looking only for a quick fix and not really able to hear anything else we might offer. And sometimes, maybe to save the life of a dog, the quick fix is exactly the right thing to offer.

When I'm faced with this kind of situation, I first try to determine what commitment—and capability—the owner has to keeping the dog (or to keeping it alive). If the commitment is not there, I recommend rehoming the dog, knowing that this owner will be unlikely to follow my suggestions, whether I choose the management or the training path. But if I find out that the owner is committed, I see it as my professional responsibility to teach not only the dog but also—maybe especially—the owner about how to change the dog's behavior and not just her environment.

Good teaching is about using all our skills, knowledge, and experience to offer our students leadership and not just instruction. Instead of just providing answers—the quick-fix approach—it's also our job to ask them questions like: "Have you tried...?" and "What would happen if you...?" and "How about considering...?" These are the mind-opening, reframing questions for which our students really come to us, even though they may not know it at the time.

"Fixing" the problem for the human student is much like doing management for the dog. The instructor takes responsibility, and the student can simply—and passively—comply. But the principles of learning apply equally to our human students as to their canine companions. What's good for the dogs is also good for the humans! As we instructors strive to do our very best work, we must give strong consideration to training our students, and not just managing them. In many more cases than we might imagine, students (like their dogs!) can learn and change their behavior. All we have to do is give them the tools and the opportunity.

My appreciation goes to Shirley Chong, who inspired this article, and to the trainers quoted here for their permission to use their stories.

Recommended Reading

Chong, M. Shirley

2001   The Clicker Cookbook: A Step by Step Guide to Beginning Manners.

An excellent book for beginners, designed for people to use by themselves if they don't have a competent clicker-training instructor. Comes with a second booklet, Appendix A & B, that contains suggested training schedules and forms for keeping a training log.

Hetts, Suzanne, Ph.D.

1999   Pet Behavior Protocols: What to Say, What to Do, When to Refer.

Although this book is written primarily for canine behavior consultants, it contains clear and helpful information for everyone. See especially Hetts' discussion of "counterconditioning" on p.42-43.

CHAPTER 8
Understanding Our
Problem-Solving Styles

I nstructors are very good at figuring out how to train dogs. We know how to try something, observe the effect, and then, if it's not what we want, try something different. We're not nearly as good, though, at training our human students. Maybe that's because dogs are easier to train. Certainly, humans are more complex animals. But is that really the reason? I think there's a better explanation.

We don't always use our dog-training skills to solve problems for our human students because our own unique problem-solving style can get in the way. It's easier to detach ourselves from the dogs than from the people in class. When it comes to people, our own "people-ness" gets stirred into the communication mix— and sometimes stirs up a batter that isn't what we had in mind!

Each of us has our own personal style of problem-solving. It's important to know what that is—and also to be aware that other people are different in how they deal with difficulties.

These individual differences in problem-solving style are a favorite and ongoing research topic for psychologists. One of the most useful models they've proposed is based on how we take in information and then make decisions based on that information. And what is good problem-solving, after all, if not this combination of observation and action?

80

If you've ever been through career counselling, you've probably encountered the Myers-Briggs Type Indicator model. This is a questionnaire, followed by an interpretation by a qualified professional, designed to help you recognize your own preferences in how you perceive the world and make choices. The psychologist David Keirsey simplified the richness of the Myers-Briggs Type model to build his own very useful model of Temperament. His model says that there are four basic Temperaments, or, for our purposes, problem-solving styles. Each one emphasizes different aspects of problem-solving, based on two important components of the process: how we gather information, and how we use that information to make decisions.

As dog trainers, we're doing this all the time. We observe the dog's behavior (gathering information) and then make appropriate adjustments in our training strategy (making decisions based on that information). In other words, we're constantly problem-solving. That's why I think it's worthwhile to become more aware of our own individual preferences in how we do this—our problem-solving styles.

I've adapted Keirsey's model of Temperaments to our own needs as instructors and come up with my own names for the four "Instructor Temperaments:" the Intellectual, the Cheerleader, the Organizer, and the Jiggler. Let's see how these might play out in a typical class situation. Let's say you've been teaching Loose-Leash Walking for three weeks now, and they're just not getting it. What to do?

The Intellectual

If your own personal preference leans towards information, you might decide to rewrite the handout so that it's "clearer." Words, concepts, and abstract ideas are very important to you. You put a high value on clarity and elegance of verbal expression. You love to design new teaching methods—and tend to lose interest when it comes to actually trying them out! You live in your head and in the future. You love to make plans, to strategize, to create. Many people see you as a visionary. You're the one who gets the idea to start a new obedience school. And you leave it to others to implement the idea in all its messy and concrete details!

The Cheerleader

If your own personal preference leans towards motivating people, you might decide to play a game or have a contest in class. You'll think of ways to encourage people to practice more at home— maybe hand out chocolates to the students who have made the most progress during the week. You're very people-oriented, and your teaching style is usually dramatic and dynamic, incorporating stories and metaphors to help students get the idea. You take it personally when people miss a class, and your greatest joy is seeing your students build better relationships with their dogs. You think of Loose-Leash Walking as a couple of friends taking a walk together, and you don't worry too much about an occasional tight leash.

The Organizer

If your own personal preference leans towards structure, you might divide the class into small groups to work on walking, or set up a gated ring in which students can practice individually. You're a very practical and realistic person who lives in the here-and-now. Time and space are real and important to you and offer many possibilities for problem-solving. You have your feet on the ground and take in information through your five senses. You like to work with concrete specifics, building your lesson plans with great attention to detail. Your classes always start and end on time. And you care a lot about how tight that leash gets!

The Jiggler

If your own personal preference leans towards playfully working outside the rules, you might hold the leash while a student is working on Loose-Leash Walking (because "the rules" don't say who has to hold the leash!). Or you might tell the student to run away from his dog (because "the rules" don't say that the dog can't rush to catch up!). Or you might suggest that the student walk backward, with the dog moving forward and following a treat in her hand (because "the rules" just say that they should both be walking in the same direction!) In other words, you like to jiggle the system, find out where the boundaries lie, and stretch them a bit. For you, a day without a problem to solve or a fire to fight is like a day without sunshine. You love to tell a joke to make a point, and April Fool's Day holds special delight for you!

Which is Best?

Which of these problem-solving styles is the best? Well, that depends! If your students are very enthusiastic and willing to do their homework but still aren't getting it, then more Cheerleading will probably only frustrate them. Instead, they might need the Intellectual's rewritten homework sheet, or the Organizer's suggestion to train in five two-minute sessions each day for a week. On the other hand, the students may be feeling overwhelmed with paper—those infamous class manuals!—and really appreciate the Jiggler's simple, fresh, and immediate approach to the problem.

Now here's the dilemma. We need all four problem-solving styles to teach well, but each of us has a natural preference for one of them and might even feel uncomfortable with some of the others. But comfortable or not, each of us has the capability to function in all four modes. The key, then, is to learn how to identify which approach is needed in any given class situation—in other words, to step outside the boundaries of our own natural preferences. Easier said than done! Like training dogs, it takes awareness and practice to reshape our problem-solving skills to the needs of the moment.

Assume That We're All Unique

Just as you have your own unique preference for one of the problem-solving styles, so does each student in your class. You respect the uniqueness of your canine students, even in little things like their preferences in training treats. Why not expect differences among your human students as well? And just as with dogs, the only way to know what those human preferences are is by carefully observing each student's responses to your instructions. If you get the famous Glazed Look, chances are good that your communication with that student is not working well.

So, what to do? My solution to the problem is to use all the styles when I teach and pay attention to the responses of each individual student. If I see confusion, I can zoom in and work with that student individually for a minute. I usually do this as a kind of public demonstration for the entire class because—who knows?—my "individual" consulting might be just the ticket for another student as well.

Let's go back to the loose-leash-walking problem. First, I ask everyone to show me what they've got so far. As they struggle with the exercise, I try to identify, in my own mind, some possible sources of difficulty. But that information won't help if I can't communicate it to my students. That's when I bring out all my Instructor Temperaments, one at a time.

I might, for example, put my Intellectual to work first by explaining to the class that walking on leash in a controlled way is not a natural behavior for a dog, and that's why it takes some time to teach it. I also remind students that most dogs are faster-moving than most humans (as if they didn't know that!), and that's why it's important to anticipate the tightening of the leash and "catch the dog doing it right" with a positive reinforcer.

Then, I might bring my Cheerleader into play by pointing out that a dog who can walk nicely on leash has much more freedom because he will not interfere with others. I'm hoping that this concern for other people and dogs in public places will be a strong motivator for my students who are themselves Cheerleader Temperaments. And, of course, that word "freedom" really rings resoundingly with these students who love to find safe ways to unleash the "free spirit" that they see in their dogs.

My Organizer might show up next, making a list on the chalkboard of all the steps in the training progression of loose-leash walking—also specifying the number of repetitions for each training session, and the number and duration of training sessions per day for each step. I might also make this list a separate handout to give the students.

And I would definitely invite my Jiggler to join in the fun by pretending I'm the dog to my assistant's "handler" and performing a silly little routine showing a Before (training) and After (training) picture. Sometimes, when my Jiggler (and the class) really gets going, I'll even play both roles myself! Of course, this is not necessarily the order of styles I mobilize every time.

And sometimes, if I think the entire class is having a specific problem, I might need only one or two of my Instructor Temperaments to reach everyone quickly. For example, if I notice students unwittingly luring their dogs by holding a treat in their left hands, all I need is my Organizer to step in and say "Put your left hand at your belt buckle as you walk, and bring it down again to deliver the treat after you click."

Or I might call on my Jiggler to bring this unintentional luring to my students' awareness by making it worse. I might ask everyone to see if they can use a food lure to move their dogs into various positions in front of them, to circle around them in both directions, to move through a spiral of Figure 8, to jump up, to lie down, to "say Yes" (a lured nod of the head), and to "say No" (another head movement). They have a grand time playing with their dogs, and the message is clear and lasting.

Whichever style I use to make my point, I always check to find out if I've succeeded. How? By asking the class—"Is that clear?" or "What questions do you have?" At this point, I might get some final, lingering, "I've almost got it, but" comments or questions. These are usually very easy and quick to resolve.

Come to think of it, maybe our human students are, in fact, easier to train than our canine students. The dogs just can't answer those questions directly, and that's why we instructors have gotten so good at training dogs. We've learned to observe and rely on their non-verbal behavior to tell us when we're not getting through. What we need to work on now is getting better at communicating with those complex human creatures.

Recommended Reading

Keirsey, David

1998   Please   Understand   Me   II: Temperament,
Character, Intelligence

This is an expanded version of Keirsey's first book (with Marilyn Bates) that was published in 1978. A comprehensive and very readable explanation of Keirsey's model of Temperaments

Myers, Isabel Briggs (with Peter B. Myers)

1980   Gifts Differing.

It was Myers who made C.G. Jung's psychological work popular in the United States and inspired Keirsey and many others. Her Myers-Briggs Type Indicator (MBTI), validated through research by the prestigious Educational Testing Service, is now widely used in schools, corporations, and other settings.

Sir Guthrie of Drumderfit(edited by Jean M. Kummerow, Ph.D.)

1989   T.I.P. - Type Indicator for Pets.

And just for fun, this little booklet presents the tongue-in-cheek version of the Myers-Briggs Type Indicator for pets. Kummerow is a psychologist, well-known for her work with the MBTI. The booklet is available from Martin-McAllister Consulting Psychologists in Minneapolis, MN, 612-338-84761.

CHAPTER 9
Designing an Effective Training Place

For the first 30 years or so of my adult professional life, it didn't matter to me where I worked, as long as I was doing the work I loved. So, for example, for four miserable years I lived in a town in the Northeast that shall remain nameless but that

we wryly called the "armpit of the country." It had the dubious virtue of being one of the few places in the United States that doctors recommended to their dangerously sun-reactive patients. I had just started my first real, post-doctorate university- teaching job, and I was thrilled to be doing what I had been dreaming of for years. The awful climate didn't bother me in the least.

My actual office, though small, was a huge step up from the space I had occupied in my previous, part-time teaching job. In that one, I did not have an office at all but only part of a desk that was located in a large room with other "junior faculty" and their desks. I was allocated the top drawer, plus the use of the desk during the daytime, while my desk "partner" had the bottom drawer and used the desk when he came in to teach night classes. But even then, I was thrilled to be teaching and would have been happy even without that single drawer.

It was only much later, when I finally found what turned out to be my university home where I taught for 14 years, that I began to pay attention to my work space. I began to notice how I always arranged that space to reflect my beliefs about teaching.

First, I realized that I was definitely an "open door" kind of professor. My first priority was my students. When they wanted to see me, I was available. Period. My own class preparation and research had to take place on my own time—evenings and weekends—and most often at home rather than at my university office. One of the concrete ways in which I communicated my availability to students was by positioning my desk so that, when I was sitting at it, my back was never to the door of the office.

I also became aware of how I liked to arrange the furniture in my office. My desk was always against a wall, with my own chair in the usual place behind the desk and an additional chair to the side of the desk. I did not see any value in separating myself physically from my students or hiding behind a desk.

Bookcases were rare and highly valued pieces of furniture at the university, and I did everything I could to have enough for my own small library. I made sure that at least one of the bookcases was placed as a sort of privacy wall between the student's chair and the office door and hallway. This arrangement reflected my understanding that not all my conversations with students were about arcane aspects of theory but many were also about very personal matters—issues with parents and boyfriends, dilemmas about career planning, personality conflicts with other faculty, difficulties with developing good study habits, and so on. My students appreciated that little bit of privacy in an otherwise very public place.

When I first started teaching dog-training classes, I was in the same fantasy fog about the training place itself. I just loved what I was doing—as I still do—and the physical surroundings seemed not to matter at all, either to my happiness or to my students' success. I taught wherever anyone would let me teach. That included a long list of inappropriate and even bizarre training places. Let me describe just a few of them, to give you an idea of my state of mind in those days.

I taught in basements with pipes that leaked water over large areas of the concrete floor. Above our training place, a children's aerobics class met and sounded like the proverbial herd of elephants. I was very fortunate that there were no sound-phobic dogs in those classes.

I've already described my experiences teaching in parks and in a church lobby (in Chapter 6, talking about the importance of paying attention to Context).

Probably the most outrageous environment in which I taught a (fortunately) one-time workshop was a park. The group that sponsored the workshop had reserved one of the wooden huts. Things started out very well—in spite of the plague of mosquitoes that swarmed in the room. Until a thunderstorm blew in and the lights went out. You know how dark it gets during a heavy storm. Did that stop me? No way! The workshop went on!

I'm happy to report that I know better these days. Maybe that's the best you can ever say about learning from experience. What I know now is that the physical environment of the training place really does make a difference. It's worth putting some effort into doing whatever I can to make it more suitable for teaching and more consonant with my own methods and beliefs about teaching people and their dogs.

This morning, I walked into my training room and saw it through the eyes of my students. The room is not very large (only 20' by 30'), and it has no windows. But the ceiling is high enough to give the room a spacious feeling.

The walls of my training room are raw wood—but they're covered with various functional and ornamental objects. Two of the walls are partially lined with mirrors. These support my efforts to teach my students that their dogs can be trained to respond to cues even without direct eye contact. No more "She can only sit when she's right in front of me." My students can give their cues and watch their dogs in the mirrors. And, of course, my competition students also benefit from the mirrors since they can really see if a Front or a Finish is straight, and they can reinforce that behavior with perfect timing. My students enjoy the Stephen Huneck prints (for more information, visit his website: <www.huneck.com> that hang above the mirrors, the colorful posters, the snapshots of Pet Partners teams visiting nursing homes, and the dog-related cartoons that I collect and post on a small bulletin board. They are duly impressed by my own dog's "trophy room"—part of a wall on which I've arranged his many obedience-trial ribbons and trophies. They learn something about my qualifications by seeing my various certificates framed and hung on one wall: NADOI (National Association of Dog Obedience Instructors), IAABC (International Association of Dog Behavior Consultants), and a few others. And, by looking at several handmade posters, they can be reminded at a glance of some of the basic principles of training, such as "Catch Your Dog Doing It Right!"

I limit my classes to eight teams, and I seat them along two walls, in white plastic garden chairs with a wall hook next to each one. The dogs can be tethered to the wall hooks to do certain exercises, so that the handler is not tempted to use leash pressure as a substitute for good training practices.

Perfect? Not quite. Central heating and air conditioning and indoor plumbing would bring the building closer to my heart's desire. But, barring that, I do have a wonderful training place that expresses and enhances my training philosophy and methods.

You don't have to remind me how lucky I am to have my own training place. I know it! But what about other instructors? I decided to do a little survey to find out how some of my colleagues around the country are managing their physical environments.

My survey respondents teach in a variety of settings, including: a horse barn, a community center, an outdoor fenced area at a veterinary clinic, a shelter or humane society, a daycare facility, a boarding kennel, and the dog food aisle of a pet superstore. Only a few of my surveyed colleagues own (or are now building) their own training place. Most of them either beg, borrow, or rent.

Even greater is the variety of things my colleagues could do without in their present training places:

- Horse poop on the floor
- Poor lighting
- Bad acoustics, due to hard wall and floor surfaces, and a high ceiling, which cause the barks to reverberate harshly and the instructor's voice to get lost in the din
- Minimal parking, in a sort of seedy area of town (next door to a busy tattoo parlor!)
- The chaos/distraction of students' dogs having to pass by a group of daycare dogs (who are waiting to be picked up before closing time) as they enter the building

And, to cap it all off:
- Bad weather and dangerous roads
- Bookkeeping
- The IRS!

And now let's look at the combined wish list of my respondents—things they dream of having in their ideal training place:

- 10,000 square feet
- Impact-resistant, non-skid floor that's easily cleaned
- Good lighting, including natural light
- Tethering stations, widely spaced around the perimeter of the room
- Portable, lightweight barriers to divide the room into various configurations
- Wall space for posters, training hints, etc.
- Storage space for equipment
- Office/display area that keeps the computer safe from dust and dog hair
- Public bathroom
- Audio-visual system to show commercial videos and to videotape students so as to provide them with feedback and measure progress
- Separate, furnished "room" for "life training", to simulate a household situation
- Separate, small space, attached to the main training room, with a "Dutch" half-door, for playtimes and and for training small or nervous dogs/pups. This way they could stay in the action, but have a feeling of security.
- Easy access to a secure outdoor area that has a comfortable surface, some shade, and is easily cleaned
- Expansive grassy area for agility training, with a retractable roof for inclement weather)

And, last but not least:

- Very wealthy investors who would finance the instructor but allow her to conduct classes in her own way!

Some of my respondents let their imaginations fly high. For example, Joyce Clark, who currently teaches at a humane society, writes:

"If I were able to redesign my training room, I would have colorful posters with the mantras of reinforcement-based training such as "reinforcement strengthens behavior." I would want to have bulletin boards with pictures of recent graduates, articles that pertain to dogs and training, information about various dog sports, and details about upcoming classes, seminars, etc. I would like to have a seating-area bench built into the wall. It would be tall and deep enough to have crate-like spaces built in underneath for quick and easy doggie dens. And I would love to have a small kitchen area with a sink, fridge, etc."

Laura Van Dyne is actually in the process of building her ideal training place, on her own property. Here's how she describes it:

"The building is the size of a 2-car garage. Windows on the south wall only, so that I get lots of light but still have wall space for hanging things. Folding chairs that I can remove from the floor and hang on the walls. Stations for each team with a secure tether in the wall for the dog. Visual blockages for eye-contact barkers. These will be portable and will also hang on the wall when not in use. A toilet. Mirrors on the walls. And the whole inside painted white to keep it bright."

Janet Smith has already built her training place. Here's her description:

"It's a huge, converted garage, approximately 3000 square feet. This indoor 'gym area' functions well for classes up to about 9 dogs. The walls are OSB board on the lower section (easy to clean), the floor is concrete, painted with an epoxy containing silica sand for traction. We've painted fun dog graphics/artwork on the walls. The space is bright and well illuminated with sound/noise control panels

hanging from the ceiling. We have a public restroom, washtubs, a reception/retail area, and an office. The building has several doors so that I can have one group entering and the previous class exiting through a different door. This is great! Really helps with the crowded, posturing chaos that you often see at single entrance/exit areas. We have chairs where students and their guests can sit. Outdoors, we have two separate fenced areas, one grass and one pea stone."

How does this fit with her teaching style and methods? "*The happy, friendly graphics on the walls lend a sense of humor and fun.*

My training style is fun! The whole atmosphere of the building is bright and friendly with a touch of humor. I like to think that is the way I teach."

Kathy Sdao used to rent space at a doggie daycare center, after hours and she describes it this way:

"*The doggie daycare is about 1200 square feet. It has a linoleum floor (yuk) and concrete walls (yuk again). The space is divided by 8' high chain-link fencing into 3 main areas. There is ample storage space in a back room and a conveniently located restroom and sink area. Wall decorations are minimal, but there are lots of toys and children's plastic play equipment (slides, tunnels, benches).*"

In spite of the unpleasant basics—and what could be more basic than floors and walls—Kathy found ways to make the most of the space in order to further her teaching goals. She wrote: "*The 3 separate areas are convenient for practicing exercises in small groups (one or two dogs) so that even beginning dogs can work off-leash. It also gives us an easy way to let shy dogs have their own space for the first class or so, until they get acclimatized to the new surroundings.*"

Nowadays, Kathy is thrilled to be teaching in a brand-new, 18,000 square foot, indoor arena that is carpeted with super-high-tech "Dream Turf." And, just in case you're wondering what it's like to teach classes in the dog food aisle of a superstore, here's Katy Donahue-Cavazos to tell us about some of the surprising advantages (and not-so-surprising disadvantages):

"Teaching in a store presents its own set of advantages and disadvantages. While customers coming and going do distract the dogs (and sometimes the handlers), the dogs do get used to them eventually and learn to pay attention to their handlers better. Other distractions include chew toys, such as rawhides, basted bones, and the bulk cookie display which I refer to as the 'buffet'.

"Bags of dog food or kitty litter can also be distracting, yet they provide unique teaching opportunities. I was once teaching at a superstore where dog food was stored on pallets, high up on shelves, before being put on display. In the middle of class one evening, a bag broke open, raining kibble on the group. 'Kibble from heaven' provided some unexpected and free treats for the students once we got past the shock of having it actually coming down practically on top of us.

"Teaching in a store also offers the advantage of publicity. Potential students see the classes being taught, stop to watch, and occasionally ask questions during classes. Again, this could be seen as a distraction, or it can be turned into a teaching opportunity. Students get a chance to work with their dogs in the presence of unexpected distractions. And those 'distractions' can turn into future students.

"The one problem that bothers me most about teaching in a store is unattended children. Kids are naturally attracted to the dogs, but they don't seem to realize that these dogs are in a class. I have often had to stop teaching in order to instruct the children on the proper way to approach strange dogs. Again, turning a disadvantage into something of an advantage!

"I used to take my shyest dog to class, both to socialize him and to use him as a demonstation dog. He was excellent as a demo

dog because he did everything in slow motion, and students could see every step of the process easily. (I joked that he'd been specially trained to work in slo-mo, but the reality of it was that that was just who he was.) He's a beautiful dog and store customers would constantly stop to admire him. Children especially would approach, usually at a run, and I'd always have my stock speech ready for them: 'I'm glad you would like to pet my dog, but he's very frightened, and, while he's never bitten anyone before, I'd really hate for you to be the first.' That would at least slow them down. I could then discuss how to approach a dog correctly, using a more kid-friendly dog from the class. That made for a good demonstration for my students on how to handle unwanted attention as well as how to approach strange dogs."*

Some of us are lucky enough to have our own training places that we can furnish and decorate as we wish. But even if we don't have that luxury, there are things we can do to the physical environment that will enhance our teaching and our students' learning. I've certainly gotten some great ideas from my survey respondents, and I hope you have too.

And, in the final analysis, what really matters is not where we teach, but what and how—and even why we're teaching. Jan Gribble, who gives classes at various locations, wherever "enough interest exists to offer a class," makes this interesting point:

"While a permanent location to use as a training site certainly has a lot of attractions, I don't think it's possible to say what constitutes an 'ideal' training place. If you pay attention to adapting your classes to the location, I believe it's possible to offer classes in a wide variety of locales. Sometimes this is even preferable, since it makes classes more accessible to those within the community."

My sincere appreciation to the following trainers who participated in this survey and graciously allowed me to use their comments:

Katherine Bryce, The Family Dog, Santa Fe, NM

Joyce Clark, Longmont Humane Society, CO

Katy Donahue-Cavazos, Pet Dog Trainer, Albuquerque, NM

Helix Fairweather, Clicker Agility Instructor, Turner, OR

Jan Gribble, ABC Dog Training, Albuquerque, NM

Don Hanson, Green Acres Kennel Shop, Bangor, ME

Doug Johnson, Good Dog Behavioral Training, Salt Lake City, UT

Kathy Sdao, Bright Spot Dog Training, Tacoma, WA

Janet A. Smith, Good Dog! Training, Okemos, MI (suburb of Lansing)

Laura Van Dyne, The Canine Consultant, Carbondale, CO

CHAPTER 10
How to Read a Feedback Form

Twenty-five years ago, I learned some important lessons about feedback that I'll never forget. I was team-teaching a 5-day workshop that I had designed with

my two colleagues, Jerry and Don. It was an unconventional and very intense workshop, and we had really put our hearts into it deeply.

The morning after the workshop ended, the three of us finally allowed ourselves to look at the feedback forms we had received from our 20 students. I remember sitting on the floor in the hotel room, reading quietly and passing forms to each other. After we had all read all the forms, there was a heavy silence in the room. Finally, Don said: "What did we do wrong?" Jerry and I knew exactly what he was referring to.

In those days, we were very scientific about how we solicited feedback from students. In this case, we had started the form with an "Overall Evaluation" where students could mark whichever one of the five categories best described their feelings about the course. Nineteen of the twenty students had marked the highest category, "Most profound educational experience I've ever had." A single student had marked the second highest category, "One of the most profound educational experiences I've ever had."

99

The three of us spent the next full hour discussing that one check mark. Was the exercise we had designed for the first day too stressful? Was Don's lecture on the second day too dry? Had we assigned this student to an incompatible sub-group? Should we have been aware of his dissatisfaction earlier in the week so that we could have done something about it? Or was the workshop just not as coherent and effective as we had hoped? And we went on and on and on like this—until suddenly Jerry said: "Wait a minute! What are we doing?" Another deep silence, as Don and I ever so slowly came out of our self-deprecating trances. And then we all burst out laughing. When the three of us get together today, twenty-five years after that important moment, we still laugh.

What did I learn from this experience? First and maybe most important, I learned how much value I place on what my students think. That's one of those Good News/Bad News items. The Good News is that I really want to reach my students, and what they think matters to me. The Bad News is that I can't possibly reach them all, no matter how hard I try or how competent I am, because they bring different histories, needs, and capabilities to a learning experience. So it's inevitable that some of the feedback I receive will be less positive than I would like.

But just hold on there a moment! Do I really consider as "less positive" a comment that my class was only one of the most profound educational experiences that a student has ever had? And there's my second important learning. Let's put this thing in perspective! Jerry always reminds me that rankings and percentages are relative to the activity. For example, if a baseball player makes a hit 30% of his times at bat, that's considered excellent. If we were talking about a fielder catching 30% of the balls hit to him, though, we could bet that he wouldn't last long.

So, translating back to teaching, if 95% of our students said that we were supercalifragilisticexpialidocious, and 5% rated us only as almost the best thing since sliced bread, I'd say (now, with my added years of wisdom) that we were doing pretty well.

This is all very clear and obvious—until you find yourself in the situation. Some instructors give too much importance and too much energy to the one student who seems less happy. Why do we do this when we know that we're depriving so many other students of our gifts—students who are ready and willing to receive them? And why do we remember the negative comments far longer than the positive ones? In short, how can we learn to receive feedback so that we can really use it to enhance our teaching?

First, let me offer some simple, mechanical answers to this question. I started out designing feedback forms for my classes that would have easily met even the rigorous standards of the American Psychological Association. I offered my students lists of word choices (for example, Helpful vs. Waste of Time), 5-degree scales (moving from Agree Strongly to Disagree Strongly), and very specific questions such as "Did the instructor speak clearly?" These feedback forms took a lot of time to design and very little time (or thought) for my students to fill out.

Gradually, my feedback forms changed from tight and regimented and numerical to open-ended and subjective and personal, including such questions as "What did you like about the class?" An earlier version of that question, in my more "scientific" days, was "What one thing did you like best about the class?" I soon realized that I was unnecessarily restricting my students' expression and cutting myself off from lots of useful information. Today, I favor the Blank Piece of Paper as my feedback form, and I invite my students simply to "give me feedback about the class." Open-ended feedback forms like these satisfy my need for information and positive reinforcement (and who doesn't need that at the end of a class?) as well as satisfying my wish that the students continue their learning by reflecting on the class and writing me feedback about it.

But no matter what kind of feedback form I use, the Morning After always arrives, and I sit down to read them. I've come a long way from that memorable Morning After with Jerry and Don. Still, though, I sometimes need a little guidance as I read feedback or, for that matter, when I receive it in any form, including spoken comments or questions from my students. I often find this guidance in the work of Virginia Satir, especially her Interaction Model. Satir worked daily with families in crisis. It was crucial for her clients to understand something about communication. The Interaction Model is Satir's analysis of what happens inside a person who is receiving feedback.

The model describes the cascade of feelings and thoughts that are triggered by the feedback, all the way from the comment itself to the response that the recipient finally makes. This cascade happens in the blink of an eye, and, before I know it, I've said or done something that I may deeply regret later on. The triggering comment might be criticism or praise—or even just a casual remark made with no particular intent at all. In fact, the trigger might even be non-verbal—a smile, a gesture, or a movement. What matters is what I do with that bit of feedback. Let's take a simple example and follow it through the model.

Step 1: Sensory Intake

A student arrives 20 minutes late. I'm in the middle of demonstrating to the class how to teach a dog to stop jumping on people, and we're just beginning to make some progress. Out of the comer of my eye, I see Gloria and her dog Rudy come into the training hall. I hear a rustle as they settle in—Gloria peeling off her jacket, disentangling herself from Rudy's leash, laying his blanket on the floor, pouring water into his little dish, dropping her class manual on the floor, gathering up the loose sheets that fell out of it, breathing loudly all the while, and finally sitting back in her chair with a heavy sigh.

Step 2: Meaning

My mind starts to interpret the sensory data. There are any number of meanings I might make of Gloria's late arrival. Here are just a few possibilities.

1. She was stuck in traffic or had to work late.
2. She hates the class, and this is another sign of her avoidance.
3. She loves the class and wouldn't miss it for anything, even on a day when she's had to work late and is exhausted.
4. She's had a discouraging week of training with Rudy and really didn't want to come at all.

Notice that my first interpretation is quite impersonal and has nothing to do with me or my class. My other three interpretations, however, amount to feedback that I imagine Gloria is giving me. Is it actually Gloria's feedback? The only way I could know for sure would be to ask her, and that's always a reasonable path to take—especially if I don't like what I think I'm hearing!

Step 3: Feeling

What I feel at this moment depends on Step 2—the meaning I've given to the event. For example, if I interpreted Gloria's lateness as a consequence of a traffic jam, I might feel sympathy. ("That's too bad. I know what it's like to fight my way through traffic to get somewhere.") If, on the other hand, I interpreted it as the result of her discouragement, I might feel guilt. ("I didn't do a good job last week explaining the homework.")

Step 4: Feeling About the Feeling

This is where things can get sticky. For example, my feeling of guilt might lead me to a feeling of anger. ("It's not my fault. Why didn't she just call me during the week when she was having trouble?")

Remember the old joke about the motorist, driving in the country late at night, who runs out of gas? He starts walking down the road, hoping to find a farm house where he can use the phone to get help. It's a long walk, and he has lots of time to think. Worrying about how the farmer will take to being awakened so late by a complete stranger, he starts to rehearse the conversation. At first, he's apologetic and pleasant but gradually, as his worry and frustration about his dilemma builds, he becomes more and more agitated. Finally, when he reaches a house and the farmer opens the door, the motorist bursts out in anger at him: "Who needs your stupid phone anyway!" Next time you tell that joke, you can explain that it's about the Feeling About the Feeling!

If I've reached Step 4, the chances are good that I'm feeling threatened and rapidly losing my self-esteem. But it's possible to skip this step entirely. Starting from a different feeling—for example, sympathy for Gloria's plight—I might have simply accepted that her lateness had nothing to do with me or how she felt about the class. Instead of feeling threatened, I might have just continued teaching.

Step 5: The Survival Rule

Having reached Step 4, though, I do feel threatened. Instead of staying in the here-and-now—maybe by making a mental note to ask Gloria, at the right moment, how her training week had gone—I'm likely to disappear into a there-and-then. For example, I might recall how guilty I felt, as a child, when I was late coming home from school. I might remember how suspicious my parents were when I told them I had just been talking to a friend and had lost track of time. I might relive my own secret feelings of anger at my parents for doubting me. So, instead of being a competent obedience instructor teaching a class, I've become an eight-year-old child again, hopelessly lost in an emotional turmoil. I've been trapped by some survival rule from the past—a rule that might have been useful when I was eight but is now only a hindrance to me. In this case, for example, it might be something like "I must always please everyone." If Gloria was having trouble with her training this week, then it must be my fault. And if that's the case, then something terrible will happen because I've violated this ironclad rule.

Let me be clear, at this point, that very little of this articulation is conscious during the event. It all happens very quickly and with great subtlety. We could not live in the world if all these feelings and thoughts occurred at the level of consciousness. But they do occur. Anyone who has ever experienced a Feeling About a Feeling will know what I mean. It's not rational, it doesn't make sense, and it's not even in our awareness at the time. And that makes it even more dangerous, as we'll see in a moment.

Step 6: The Defense

Once a survival rule has been activated, I feel I must defend myself—even though the "threat" might be only in my perception and interpretation of the event. And once I'm in defense mode, everything goes haywire. I'm functioning on some primitive level of automatic-pilot, just trying to survive.

Step 7: The Response

How I respond to the event is a direct outcome of all that's happened inside me during the split second that this process takes. Let's say that my interpretation of Gloria's lateness has kicked me into guilt, then into anger, then into a survival rule that says I must please everyone, and finally into defense mode. My response might be a sarcastic comment ("Well. It's about time.") Or I might carefully ignore Gloria for the rest of the hour. Or I might try to "make amends" by paying a lot more attention to Rudy than any other dog in the class.

These are not conscious decisions but, instead, are driven by the cascade of feelings that has swept me away. Once caught in the cascade, I am no longer a free agent, acting out of choice. I'm a prisoner of my lowered self-esteem, and none of my normal powers of insight, intelligence, and feeling are functioning.

By way of contrast, let's look at the cascade as it might have progressed from one of the other meanings I might have given to Gloria's lateness. She was stuck in traffic. I'm sympathetic. I do not experience any Feeling About my Feeling of sympathy. I do not go away in my mind to some other time and place. My self-esteem remains high, and I'm not bothered by any survival rule or the need to defend myself. My response to the event, then, might be a simple "Hi, Gloria! Hi Rudy!"

The important point here is that I do have choices. I can choose to perceive Gloria's late arrival in class as feedback about me or my class. Or I can decide that it has nothing to do with me at all. The choice I make will determine how far down the cascade of the Interaction Model I'll fall.

But what if I'm really receiving feedback—let's say, on a written feedback form at the end of the course? That's always a little more difficult because all I have is written words and no tone of voice, facial expression, or other non-verbal accompaniments that might help me understand the student's meaning. Still, though, the Interaction Model can help. Here's how to make use of the steps.

Step 1: Sensory Intake

Read the comment in question. Then read it again—and again and again. Make sure you are reading what the student wrote and not what you think is between the lines.

Step 2: Meaning

Think of at least three different interpretations of the comment, at least one of which has nothing whatever to do with you or the class. If you're still not sure you have the meaning right, go to the source. Ask the student: "I'm not sure I understand exactly what you meant when you wrote...." Put a period at the end of your statement, and wait. Allow the student to respond. Continue the inquiry for as long as you need, in order to be sure you've gotten the student's intended meaning.

Step 3: Feeling

The way you feel about the meaning is not subject to "correction." Feelings are real, natural, and visceral. All you have to do, at this step in the process, is allow yourself to be fully aware of what you're feeling. If you try to deny it, or revise it, you're simply deceiving yourself—and almost guaranteeing that you'll continue to slide down the cascade.

Step 4: Feeling about the Feeling

Once you've identified your feeling about the comment, check to see if there's a feeling about the feeling lurking inside you somewhere. If you find nothing else behind the feeling you experienced, go directly to the Response step, and do or say whatever seems most fitting and appropriate. But if you sense any discomfort at all, chances are there is something more to be uncovered. Allow that to come to awareness so that you can examine it.

Step 5: The Survival Rule

If you've uncovered a feeling about the feeling, consider the possibility that a survival rule has been activated. Realize that you're now in a different universe—the universe of self, family, and personal history. What you're experiencing at this moment has nothing to do with the comment you've just read on the student's feedback form. Instead, this is a moment of rich opportunity for you to learn more about yourself.

Step 6: The Defense

When you've identified the survival rule, think about other times and situations in which this rule has been activated. What are your characteristic coping strategies in this situation? Do you go into denial? Do you try to appease? Do you look for someone to blame? Remember that these are all natural reactions to feeling threatened. And, though they are natural, they're not necessarily the most effective ways to get untangled from the situation.

Step 7: The Response

One good thing about the Morning After when we're reading feedback forms is that we're not required to make any response at all. We can take as much time as we need to figure out what's going on and what, if anything, to do about it. (And doing nothing about it is also a possible choice.) So take that time, and get whatever support you need. Find a friend or a colleague who might help you work through the Interaction Model. Go for a walk with your dog. Listen to music. Give yourself enough time and space to understand what's happened and to integrate what you've learned.

Here are some of the responses I've made to comments on feedback forms:

- I've talked to the student to get more information.
- I've reviewed parts of the class design, revising some parts and letting others stand.
- I've offered additional private training to the student.
- I've tried some new training ideas on my own dogs.
- I've rewritten the description of the class.
- I've written an article about what I learned.

I've had lots of experience sloshing around in the cascade of the Interaction Model, even feeling, sometimes, that I never wanted to teach again. Understanding what's happening does not mean that it will never happen again. It does mean, though, that I approach the next cascade with a little more confidence, some new tools, and some strategies for getting through it. Once I know that I won't drown, I can use the experience—yes, even the pain of it—to become a better instructor.

Recommended Reading

Seashore, Charles N., Edith Whitfield Seashore, Gerald M. Weinberg

1992   What Did You Say?: The Art of Giving and Receiving Feedback.

A delightful book influenced heavily by the work of Virginia Satir. The authors are organizational consultants, but this book is for everyone to read and enjoy.

CHAPTER 11
A Toolkit for Maintaining Self-Esteem

Every day I receive a train-ing bag full of mail-or-der catalogs. No, make that a truckload full! One of these is called the "Self Care" cat-alog. It's kind of a New Age collection of copper bracelets, magnetic bedpads, Chinese foot massagers, and back-ex-ercise equipment that looks like a medieval torture ma-

chine. The catalog seems to be suggesting that, if you just take care of your physical and "spiritual" needs, you'll be practicing self care. I'd like to offer a different meaning of the term: "self care" means "care of the Self." And because the most important equipment we have when we teach people how to train their dogs is our own Self, for better or for worse, we need to make sure that Self is in good condition.

What we're talking about here is the Self that contains our intelligence, our problem-solving ability, our perceptiveness, our sensitivity, and our creativity. Virginia Satir gave us the graphic and aromatic image of Self as a stewpot. Here I am, cooking up a delicious stew, and my pot is full of tasty ingredients that blend well together, send off lovely aromas, and produce an excellent dinner. Satir said that this "High Pot" image was like the feelings I have when my self-esteem is high. I know what I need in order to teach an effective class. I'm confident in my ability to design the learning process and determine the right training progressions.

I'm pleased with my competence, and I'm thoroughly enjoying myself. Doesn't that describe perfectly what it feels like to teach a really good class?

In contrast, when the stewpot is low, with just a sparse few ingredients in it, the most likely outcome will be that the stew will burn. Satir called this human condition "Low Pot." I go to class feeling unsure of myself. I wonder if I can do a good job of explaining the new training steps. I'm concerned about my students' interest in the class. I'm angry about those who haven't been training at home. Deep down, I'm not even sure that I'm really qualified to teach. All of us, regardless of how much experience we've had, have experienced these feelings. We go into a nose dive of self-doubt and our self-esteem plummets. We find ourselves being sucked into a whirlpool. The more we lose confidence, the worse we perform.

This is the moment when we need tools to maintain our self-esteem—our High-Pot state. True, sometimes magnets or massagers might be just the ticket, but most of the time those are just temporary fixes. The stew is burning and, by adding a little hot water, we're not going to make it much tastier.

What might really help, though, are some of the tools in what Satir called the Self-Esteem Maintenance Kit. When I first learned about this "toolkit," I paid very little attention. It seemed too fanciful and even downright silly, and I didn't see the relevance to my needs when I'm in a Low-Pot state. But then I found myself recalling the images and metaphors when I needed them most, and I realized the power of this visual imagery. I even began to collect tangible representations of each tool. If you're willing to play along and visualize a bit, let's rummage through the toolkit together.

Wisdom Box

The Wisdom Box is the part of me that I can consult to find out what I really want or need at this moment, even when I'm feeling confused and disoriented. To represent my Wisdom Box, I have a small, brass box, made in India and covered with beautiful filigree. My Wisdom Box has informed me, for example, that I have a headache and need to take a break from class to get an aspirin. It has also helped me know when I do not want someone to sign up for my class, even though I "should" accept all comers.

My Wisdom Box has also told me about some of my most important, long-term objectives for a class, helping me to get beyond the immediate, day-to-day routines of teaching. And sometimes my Wisdom Box gives me information about what I want without supplying any rational basis for it. For example, when I decided to shift my life to working full-time in dogs, part of me raised all sorts of questions. But my Wisdom Box knew the truth—my truth—and I listened.

Yes-No Medallion

This is the tool that reminds me that I have a choice about accepting or refusing a request. I often wear a gold chain with a beautiful little German Shepherd figure hanging from it. I rarely wear my Yes-No Medallion, but I always keep it with me in my mind. For example, when I'm asked if I'd be willing to travel to give a workshop, I consult my Wisdom Box. Am I willing? Well, not really. I've been travelling too much lately and need some time at home. Can I just say No to this flattering invitation? I can with the help of my Yes-No Medallion. And, because I'm acting out of choice rather than compulsion and because I'm in a High-Pot state, I can say No in a way that doesn't hurt the other person and doesn't prevent future invitations: "Thank you for inviting me. I feel honored. Unfortunately, it doesn't fit for me right now."

Interestingly, when I allow myself the possibility of saying No, then I am also making my Yes more genuine. When I do want to accept a student, I can say and fully mean "I'd love to have you in my class."

Wishing Wand

After consulting my Wisdom Box and maybe using my Yes-No Medallion to sift through various possibilities, I can use my Wishing Wand to ask for what I want. Many of us were raised in families where saying "I want" was mightily discouraged and even punished. Remember the old admonition: "Children should be seen and not heard." But even children have wishes and desires. The message we receive in such families is that our wishes are somehow not worthy or important. Suddenly, at the magical Age of Majority, we're supposed to be able to start expressing those wishes, after years of being told to suppress them. Many of us become adults without ever learning how to use the Wishing Wand. I must frequently remind myself that, if I don't ask for what I want, there's probably very little chance that I'll get it. Of course, asking does not come with a guarantee of receiving!

Courage Stick

My Courage Stick is what helps me move through my fears. For example, I might know exactly what I want but don't dare ask for it. Maybe I won't get it. Maybe I'll offend someone by asking. Maybe I don't even deserve it. And there goes my self-esteem down the drain! So, instead, I use my Courage Stick and go ahead and ask anyway. The Courage Stick does not eliminate the fear, but it does give me that little extra bit of support—say, to help me use my Wishing Wand—from a High-Pot place.

I had occasion to use my Courage Stick recently when I wanted to go directly into the intermediate-level workshop of a series, without first taking the prerequisite introductory workshop. With Courage Stick in hand (metaphorically), I wrote a long letter to the workshop presenter and made my best case. The answer came back "No." But I came away from the discussion feeling good that I had made a genuine effort. After all, just using my Wishing Wand doesn't guarantee success. The only positive outcome is that my self-esteem remains high—and that's a very positive outcome.

Detective Hat

The Detective Hat represents my ability to figure things out. I use my Detective Hat almost every day when I work with a student. I have it on from the first moment on the phone, when I start to take in information about the student and her dog. When I'm in a High Pot state, I use all my best interviewing skills to get the information I need to help the student. When my self-esteem is not so high—maybe I'm still recovering from the flu, or maybe I've just taught a less-than-perfect class—my Detective Hat helps me figure out what's needed.

For example, a student calls to tell me that his dog has suddenly, "inexplicably" started soiling in the house. The student sounds angry and discouraged, and, for a moment, I drop into Low Pot as I empathize with his feelings and wonder if I can help. But then I realize that I need to find out what's been going on in the household. I don my Detective Hat and begin the investigation. And—sure enough!—the student's work schedule has recently changed. Elementary, my dear Watson! It's often the Detective Hat that leads our students to believe that we perform magic!

Golden Key

The Golden Key reminds me of my ability to explore new possibilities. It allows me to open doors. A friend of mine, for example, recently used her Golden Key to find a way to keep students motivated by changing her class schedule from the conventional 8-week course to a four-week course that meets twice each week.

Another friend, realizing that many pet owners are simply unable to teach their dogs to come when called under all circumstances, decided to teach a special Recall class. Using her Golden Key, she designed it to run for several weeks, meeting in a different park each week. Using her Golden Key, she was able to consider new ways to accomplish her goals.

I used my own Golden Key not long ago when I designed a two-meeting workshop, instead of a multi-week class, to accommodate a large group of people in a local business who wanted to learn how to prepare their dogs for certification in a therapy-dog program.

The Golden Key, like any other key, also has the property that it can close doors, and that's really important because it provides a safety net. So, if we choose to open a door and don't like what we see on the other side, we can use the Golden Key to lock that door again, at least for the time being. For example, many instructors have been experimenting with holding their first class without dogs and giving people homework to do during the coming week before bringing their dogs to the second class. But what if you don't like the results of having opened that door? No problem! All you have to do is use your Golden Key to close that door. "This didn't work very well. But maybe I'll try it again some other time."

Heart

The Heart is a recent addition to my self-esteem Maintenance Kit, in the form of a big, red, velveteen, heart-shaped pin-cushion that's big enough to hold in both hands. When I hold it, I'm reminded of the warmth and compassion that I can offer my students when none of the other tools are enough. I have students who agonize over their dogs who suffer from separation anxiety, destroying the house and injuring themselves when left alone. I have students whose families have been torn apart by divorce, with each dog going to one of the spouses. I have students whose wonderful companion dogs and jogging partners are now old, arthritic, and incontinent. When I've reached the limits of my creativity and problem-solving ability, I still have my Heart to offer—and that sometimes makes all the difference.

My Heart reminds me that objectivity and detachment are not always helpful, especially when my own emotions become engaged. Instead of pretending that I feel nothing, I can participate in the sadness or frustration that my student is feeling. I can share my own personal experiences of loss or pain and communicate the important message that my student is not alone.

As you've been reading about these tools, you may have been reminded of "The Wizard of Oz." Not at all surprising, since that was Virginia Satir's inspiration for her toolkit. Remember that classic movie? The Lion wanted Courage. The Scarecrow wanted a Brain. The Tin Man wanted a Heart. They accompanied Dorothy to the Emerald City where they hoped that the famous and powerful Wizard would grant their wishes. But the Wizard turned out to be nothing more than a simple and wonderfully wise human being who understood that, by taking care of the Self, everyone could become the best they could be.

He persuaded them, too, that they already had all these qualities and simply needed reminders. As instructors, we can be our own Wizards by learning to recognize when our pot is low and knowing what we need to restore that delicious stew of knowledge and compassion.

Recommended Reading

Satir, Virginia, John Banmen, Jane Gerber, Maria Gomori

    1991   The Satir Model: Family Therapy and Beyond.

This book explains the models and techniques that Satir used in her work as a family therapist. They are just as useful to help instructors better understand themselves and their students. You'll find the description of the Self-Esteem Maintenance Kit on pages 293-297.

CHAPTER 12
A Valentine's Day Card:
Hints for Self Appreciation

February in New Mex-
ico brings us the first
inkling of spring. Tem-
peratures move up into
the 50s, and green shoots
start appearing in our gar-
dens. February was the
first time I ever saw this
wonderful state. My hus-
band and I and our two

German Shepherds drove the 1000 miles or so from our home
in eastern Nebraska to spend a week of exploration. 1 remember
the moment when I first climbed out of the van. The first thing I
noticed was that I was not shivering. The second thing I noticed
was that, even in the heart of Albuquerque, I could see mountains. And I fell in love!

During that week, I showed Sweetie at a local fun match. We
also took a tracking lesson, and I watched him track in the desert
for the first time as if he'd been doing it all his life. We visited
Linda Tellington-Jones, the founder of TTouch, and learned
some new ways to manage Honey's fear. We went on lovely, long
hikes on the ditch banks in town and in the mountains. At the
end of the week, we decided that this was the place for us and
started making plans to move to New Mexico as soon as possible.
So February has very special meaning for me.

February is also the month when, on Valentine's Day, we
declare our affection for others. Maybe it's because we're so tired

of the long, cold winter that we yearn for some warmth—at least emotional, if not physical. Why not some of that affection for ourselves? As obedience instructors, we need all the warm fuzzies we can get, whatever month it is. We step forward and put ourselves on public display, offering advice that we're not always sure will help. There are too many variables to be certain, since we're dealing with living beings, both human and canine. What works for one dog-handler team might not work for another. And we don't always know what's really going on at home with our students, nor do we always feel it's appropriate to inquire.

So, in addition to the basic set of skills we've developed and practiced, we need something more. Knowing how to train dogs and having the "people skills" that enable us to communicate with our human students is just the beginning of the art of instructing. We also need self awareness, self understanding, and self appreciation—in other words, we need our very own Valentine's Day card.

In keeping with the season, I'd like to share with you some self appreciations that were generated by a group of instructors for whom I taught a workshop a few years ago. To help them prepare for the workshop, I asked them to list what they most appreciated about themselves as instructors. I organized their responses into categories that made sense to me.

As you read—and enjoy—these self appreciations, think about which of these characteristics and skills fit for you. Which ones take higher priority for you than others? Which would you like to add to your own repertoire? What others would you list for yourself?

It may be difficult—or, at least, unfamiliar—to appreciate yourself. Our culture teaches us that self appreciation is just a step away from boasting, and boasting is a bad thing. But, in our efforts to be egalitarian and not set ourselves above others, we may be missing the point. Just look at the self appreciations offered by the instructors in my workshop. Not one of them is comparative or competitive. It's true that one instructor mentioned that her "ability to communicate has so improved," but she was using herself, in the past, as a standard for comparison. Far from being boastful, this instructor was appreciating her ability to learn and grow.

There's no question that appreciating myself can lead to knowing myself better. And knowing myself opens up the possibility of growth. So, if you're hearing your mother's voice in your head warning you about the "sin of pride," reassure her gently that this Valentine's Day card to yourself is really about learning how to become an even better instructor.

Personal Characteristics

- I'm enthusiastic, highly motivated, and committed.
- I'm intellectually inquisitive.
- I am personable and understanding—never a defeatist. There is always hope.
- I have a calm, respectful attitude.
- I like my students and their dogs.
- I'm articulate.
- I am able to view a class as a whole and as a group of individuals.
- I like the sound of my voice.
- I am a helping person.
- I have patience.
- I get a feeling of euphoria from the success of a student.
- I am detail oriented, so my students will be able to progress as far and high as they want.

- It gives me a kick to see people and dogs learning.
- I have a sincere love and affinity for dogs.

Problem-Solving Ability

- I'm a good problem solver.
- I am usually successful with individual problems. I can see what needs to be done and can offer a clear picture to help the owner do something different, if necessary. Often, I'll handle the dog myself, try the alternative until it works, so I know what the dog "feels" like. Then I can better verbalize what I want the student to do.
- I have the ability to identify and isolate causes of problem canine behavior.
- If it wasn't for my class, some dogs would have gone to the pound.

Knowledge and Continuing Education

- I am well qualified, have a lot of experience, and really know the program.
- I know what I am doing and why, and I can explain if asked. Having made numerous mistakes in the past when training my own dogs, I especially want to be able to help others avoid pitfalls. Of course, the more stumbles along the road, the more people learn.
- I am able to put people and their dogs in a position of success, thus creating a more harmonious relationship.
- I know my material and can present it well.
- I'm open minded and willing to learn from students. And I continue my education from books and seminars.

121

- My greatest joy is to continuously learn more about my subject.

Interpersonal Skills

- I like the way I interact with dogs and people.
- I appreciate my ability to handle dogs and assist their owners.
- I work well with both children and adults.
- I really enjoy working with people and their dogs— and it shows in class!
- I have patience wth "difficult" students and can usually connect with their learning style.
- I have the ability to observe and to approach people.
- I work well with a group—better than one-on-one.
- I love to teach, and it shows!
- I am flexible with people and dogs and training methods.
- I am unprejudiced. I enjoy having in my classes ordinary people with their out-of-control dogs. They get as much attention from me as the serious competition folks. Many ignore these "problem" people in their classes. After all, they're not the ones who shine in the competition ring and give their schools and instructors the reputation of Super-Dog makers!

Sense of Humor

- I have a good sense of humor and I refuse to take myself too seriously in classes. This has the effect of helping students lighten up and enjoy their dogs and training.

- I like my up attitude—keeping class fun and moving right along.
- I'm friendly, very helpful, and great at keeping everyone loose and laughing.
- I try to make class fun and a positive situation.
- I believe that my honesty with my students is very important.
- They know that, through my joking and fun making, I give each one of them all the attention and help in reaching their goals that they need— and I do mean their goals, not mine.
- I know how to keep the atmosphere light and happy and still get the work done.

Classroom Mechanics

- I know how to maintain traffic control.
- I'm good at maintaining control!
- I'm punctual—I try to start and stop on time.

Communication Skills

- I'm able to teach in a clear and concise way so that students are able to understand.
- I know how to present material in several different ways in order to find one that the student can understand.
- My ability to communicate has so improved, as well as my ability to read the handler in trouble, and the successes I'm having reinforce my confidence.
- I can listen well and offer help.
- I have a very good eye for detail and can present complicated material methodically and precisely.

- I enjoy working with beginners. They are so overwhelmed and appreciative of the often dramatic improvement in the dog's behavior when they do as instructed. It is just a delight to work with them. Of course, there are the others who are not as quickly successful due to lack of committment or lack of understanding, and these people are the spice of challenge.
- I am able to teach people and not just train dogs.

Happy Valentine's Day—every day!

My thanks and appreciation to all of you whose words I've quoted.

CHAPTER 13
What To Do About Burnout

If you're a new instructor, or if you're converting your teaching from one method to another, you probably don't know much about burnout. You might even wonder how it's possible for someone to stop loving what they love so much, as you do now. Be assured: burnout happens!

Burnout is most likely to happen in mid-career. You've been training your own dogs and teaching other people how to train their dogs for a few years now. You've developed methods that work well for both your human students and their canine partners. You've worked out the logistics of instructing— where and when to offer classes, what help you need (assistant instructors, administrative support), and the basics of classroom management. You've been doing some private training and behavior consulting. You've been giving back to the profession by volunteering your services and knowledge in various ways— helping out at the local shelter, working with new foster and adoptive "parents" of rescue dogs, or writing a column on dog training for your local newspaper.

125

You're very good at what you do, and you have quite a few years of experience under your belt. Suddenly, burnout strikes!

Here are some of the words and phrases people use to describe what burnout is like: apathy, sluggishness, lack of interest, low energy, frustration, helplessness, boredom, fatigue, hopelessness. Suddenly, teaching seems so difficult and unrewarding. Suddenly, students seem so stupid and stubborn. Suddenly, dogs seem so graceless and uneducable. A colleague of mine, seized by burnout, put it succinctly: "I'm sick and tired of teaching people how to get their dogs to stop pooping on the living room rug." This statement beautifully captures the sense of trivialization of what once seemed so important and valuable.

There are some obvious reasons why people burn out—for example, working too hard, trying to do too much, going too far beyond our own physical and emotional limitations. But I believe these are only the effects of some underlying issues that are the real source of burnout. Understanding these issues can help us understand why we overwork ourselves and drive ourselves into this unhappy place.

First, we'll look at what I call the Dreaded "Shoulds"—all the requirements and constraints that we feel are imposed on us from the outside and that eat away at our self-esteem. Then, we'll consider what happens when we get so much reinforcement— the Warm Fuzzies—that we are trapped in our own success and afraid to change. Finally, I'll suggest some ways by which we can turn all these around to our advantage—by actually cultivating the Chaos that they produce in our lives.

The Dreaded "Shoulds"

When we feel that we are being forced to do something we don't want to do, when it seems as if our options have been reduced to zero, when we cannot see a way out of what appears to be a very tight box—those are the precipitators of burnout.

Think about times when you've felt your autonomy was seriously threatened, when someone else was calling the shots—and those shots were nowhere near your own. I have colleagues, for example, who teach 12 classes a week for a school—"because you're our best instructor." Others are required by their club to accept as many as 25 students in a beginners' class—"because of our high dropout rate" (I wonder why!). Still others reluctantly take on private students whose dogs have serious aggression problems—"because there's no one else who will work with them." Now, it is possible that you'd rather be teaching classes than doing anything else, that you thrive on large classes, and that you love working with aggressive dogs. But if you're not such a person, then you've bought into some activities that will very likely lead to burnout.

I learned a lot about burnout when I was a Music major in college and dreamed of becoming a concert pianist. I auditioned for a seat in the class of a famous piano teacher, hoping to be accepted by her into the music conservatory where she taught. I failed the audition and spent the rest of my senior year in deep disappointment and depression.

Finally, I was persuaded to give up my performance ambitions and get a graduate degree in Musicology instead. Now, Musicology, the study of the history and theory of music, has as much to do with playing the piano as Vertebrate Paleontology has with training dogs. Interesting background information, yes, but a very poor substitute for hands-on training. For me, Musicology was not only second-best but last-best. Every day, in every class I attended, with every term paper I wrote, I was painfully reminded of how I wasn't doing what I really wanted to do.

When the time came to write my thesis for the degree, I had almost reached bottom. I got through it only because a good friend pointed out that actually writing the thesis could not possibly be as bad as the wretchedness I was feeling as I worried and resisted and struggled over the task. I hated every minute of it, but somehow, I managed to pull it off. And I have not played the piano, even for my own pleasure, since then. That's burnout.

My problem was rooted in the Dreaded Shoulds. I felt that I Should give up my concert ambitions because one person had rejected me as a student. I believed that I Should settle for last-best because I couldn't even consider discovering and pursuing some other dream. I thought that I Should finish what I had started, as painful as it was. I was trapped in my own Shoulds.

I've stood at the brink of burnout many times since those days. For example, when I was training my own dog with someone whose training philosophy did not fit well with my own, I was caught in the Believe-the-Expert trap. You know that one: "He's the expert, so I should do what he says." Today, when I see some of my own students falling into that trap—and I'm the "expert"—I put a hasty end to that!

Most of my students are not victims of this particular Should. In fact, many of them come to me when they find they simply can no longer go along with the methods promoted by their previous instructor. Some of them wait just a tad too long to free themselves, and then they find themselves sliding into burnout—avoiding training and maybe even resenting their dog for the guilt they experience in the grip of the Dreaded Should.

As an instructor, I've also risked burnout by agreeing to do what my best judgment told me was not right for me— for example, allowing too many students to take a class ("I Should accept everyone"), tolerating students who never did the homework ("I Should not force anyone"), using techniques I didn't care for that were required by the club I was teaching for ("I Should be flexible"), and on and on.

Unfortunately, one of the symptoms of burnout is the inability to reach out for help. That means that, when we most need emotional support and new ideas, we are least likely to look for it ("I Should be able to do it myself"). Burnout is fundamentally a state of very low self-esteem. When we're there, we see ourselves as not deserving. Asking for help and support seems, in that state of being, to broadcast our own worthlessness and incompetence.

The Warm Fuzzies

But competence itself isn't a sure cure for low self-esteem, and, curiously, it can even become a precipitator of burnout. When you're good at what you do, you usually get lots of reinforcement. You get really wonderful student evaluations. Your enrollments increase as your satisfied students spread the word. You find yourself attracting more serious and hard-working students. You get letters of grateful appreciation from students whose dog-behavior problems you've solved. You learn that you've saved the life of a dog who had been brought to you as a last resort before euthanasia.

We instructors understand that, whatever training method-ology we use, reinforcement is an important element to increase the behavior we want in our students and their dogs. Reinforce-ment is an essential part of the learning process.

If the rate of reinforcement is too low, the student and the dog don't experience enough success. As a consequence, one or both of them shut down and maybe even give up. That's why we try to keep reinforcement flowing freely in the early stages of learning, and then gradually reduce the rate as competence builds. The art of teaching really centers on knowing the "when" and the "how much" of reinforcement.

Fortunately, most instructors today understand that if students or their dogs do not get enough reinforcement for their work, they simply quit. We no longer follow the principle of "No pain, no gain" that formerly dominated dog training. We no longer believe that people or dogs necessarily learn all that much from their mistakes but, instead, that they learn more by being guided through a steady climb of tiny successes. We know that a low rate of reinforcement can lead to shutdown—in other words, burnout.

But can we give too much reinforcement? Certainly! In both situations—too little and too much reinforcement—the results are the same. Both human and dog become passive and finally just quit. They burn out even before they've moved very far along the road of learning. Whenever I hear someone talk about how their dog is "bored" with training, I suspect they're caught in the burnout web of reinforcement. The dog is not "bored" but simply no longer in the game because the rate of reinforcement is not appropriate and effective.

Exactly the same thing is true of instructors. If our competence is under- or over-rewarded, we are likely to doubt and discount the value of the reinforcement. Interestingly, this is especially true when we become really good at what we do and begin to reap the fruits of success.

Picture this. You've been teaching for several years. Your classes always fill, and your dropout rate is low. Because of the high rate of reinforcement you're getting, you begin to hesitate about changing anything in your student manual except maybe the color of the cover. You become overly sensitive to any chance comment that might be critical, and you worry about the slightest confusion a student might show in class. You begin to pick and choose students more carefully until your classes contain only well-socialized and well-behaved dogs. You become more and more risk-aversive. After all, it's working, so why change anything?

Soon, you notice that you're not looking forward to classes any more. You start criticizing and making fun of your students to your colleagues. You lose patience more easily and find yourself in a grouchy mood more often. You no longer invite colleagues to observe your classes and give you feedback. Why bother? Things are going well, and there's no need to change anything.

And yet...something is not right. You don't feel good about yourself or about your work. You might even start to have health problems, be more accident-prone, start cancelling classes more easily for "health" or "weather" reasons.

This is the sad story of burnout. Is it necessary or even inevitable? Not if you understand what's going on.

Cultivating Chaos

Virginia Satir oudined the stages of what she called the Change Model, describing how change and learning happen. To understand burnout, we need to look at the stage called Old Status Quo. This is the place where our competence and success have been well established, and all we're doing now is repeating ourselves endlessly. As dulling and depressing as it is to be in Old Status Quo, we still prefer the misery of the familiar to the uncertainty of stepping out into a new place. When we're in Old Status Quo, we'll choose pain over risk any day. The pain might be only at the level of being bored, or it might be manifested as actual physical pain or even illness. But we hang on anyway because it's tried and true and safe.

Many people remain in the Old Status Quo all their lives. They finish school, get married, find a job, and stay there forever, just counting the days till retirement. Others, though, are rudely shoved out of Old Status Quo by what Satir called a Foreign Element.

Something comes along that forces you to try something different because the risk now feels like losing everything you have. For example, suppose the owner of the wonderful training facility you've been renting for years and now consider your own suddenly decides to sell the building to an auto dealership, and you have to move. Now, that's a rude awakening! Suddenly, you become aware that you've been hanging on for a long time—and now you're being forced to let go.

Much as you would like to remain in the Old Status Quo, that decision has been taken out of your hands. You might try to hang on by negotiating with the building owner, or by begging for more time (just another 10 years!), but finally you have to face up to the Foreign Element and do something else.

And now, instead of the mind-dulling "comfort" of Old Status Quo, you're thrown into the next stage: Chaos, also known as Burnout Supreme. Nothing makes sense anymore. There are either too many or too few options out there. Every time you think you have a solution, a dozen more possibilities or doubts pop up in your mind. You feel as if you're sailing a small sailboat in the middle of a rough and stormy sea. At moments, the clouds part and the downpour stops, but then it starts again even more forcefully. You feel—well, "crazy" is a good word for the Chaos stage!

Chaos feels very different from Old Status Quo—in fact, almost the opposite. It's not dull but agitating. It's not safe but scary. It's not depressing but turbulent with energy. There is no order. You feel off balance and confused.

But look at all the new ideas floating around in the churning waves! Notice the possibilities for creativity and for letting go of old assumptions and beliefs. The worst has happened: your sailboat has been torn apart by the storm. And look at all the wonderful bits and pieces of wood, canvas, plastic, and metal that are suddenly available to you.

This is the essence and power of Chaos. It's in Chaos that we rediscover our ability to learn and grow. Chaos is where we find our willingness to risk and to play. For example, let's go back to the case of the lost training building. Hit with that Foreign Element, you might decide to take a break from teaching regular classes and try something you've been thinking about for years—maybe offering your services to a shelter and training volunteers to make dogs more adoptable—but were not free to do when you still had rent to pay on "your" building and couldn't afford the time or financial risks.

I know instructors who have found the freedom, in Chaos, to do marvelous things. Donna, for example, decided to make a professional video of her training method. Frank started teaching Tricks classes for children at the local community center. Sheryl moved seriously into training teams to do animal-assisted therapy. And Nora created a private "Dog Park" for her own students, giving them the opportunity to learn about canine behavior by observing their dogs interacting with other dogs without benefit of leashes or other human controls. As for me, I first started teaching people how to train their dogs when I was burned out on teaching university undergraduates.

All of us used Chaos to our benefit, as a way to put burnout behind us and recreate our professional lives so that we were once again making important contributions. Risk-taking, inventiveness, and learning all come out of Chaos.

Getting the Most Out of Chaos

Because burnout comes from a perceived constriction of choice—the Dreaded Shoulds—we can use Chaos to take back control of our life. The first step is to find support and practice self care.

- <u>Value yourself, your beliefs, and your ideas.</u> Avoid placating and putting the wishes of others before your own.
- <u>Trust yourself.</u> Know your bottom line, and honor it. If something isn't right for you, just say No!
- <u>Know yourself and your personal style and preferences.</u> When you take time to relax, be sure that you're really relaxing. For example, "relaxing" for me means physical activity, not "resting" (inactivity). For you, it might mean sitting down with a good novel.
- <u>Practice self care by honoring your own physical and emotional</u> <u>limitations.</u> For example, you might find qualified assistants who can take over one of your classes, or you might train an assistant to do some of your private lessons.
- <u>Take a break.</u> Getting away from the daily routine, even if it's just for a day or two, can be refreshing. Make good use of your free time to do something entirely different. And, if you don't have any free time, make some!
- <u>Actively seek support from others.</u> Talk to other trainers, exchange stories, articulate complaints, verbalize your feelings and concerns about problem dogs or handlers. And be open to ideas and suggestions that your colleagues offer. Talk and listen!
- <u>Respect your need for meaningful, appropriate, and nourishing reinforcement.</u> Remember that

reinforcement issues—for example, an excess of Warm Fuzzies—are also a breeding ground for burnout. You will be rebuilding your self-esteem.

- Remind yourself of your successes. Provide your own reinforcement by putting those "feel good" letters from satisfied students on a bulletin board, in a scrapbook, or both. And remember to look at them when you're feeling low!
- Recognize your "boredom" as Old Status Quo—and then move on. Take courage to give up the comfort of familiarity for the riskiness of growth.
- Seek out the support of people who do more than just telling you how "great" you are.
- Cultivate and cherish the Chaos in which you find yourself. Experience it as a place to restore, refresh, rebuild motivation and excitement.
- Seek out new ideas—the wilder the better. Brainstorm with friends and colleagues. And then—just try it!
- Ask for emotional support when you need it. A sounding board or a soft shoulder might be all you need.
- Learn something new, and try it out in class. Give yourself some protection by telling your students that this is a new idea. Most students really appreciate the opportunity to participate in guided experiments and will respect you for your willingness to learn.

Like many others who have experienced burnout, I know that there's no way but up from there. Even though it may feel as if the walls are closing in on me, I remind myself that burnout and its accompanying Chaos also offer possibilities and new doors to open. To find and open those doors takes awareness, understanding, courage, and support. And having been through this cycle myself, I become an even better instructor because of the help I can give my students when I see them struggling.

A special appreciation to Margery West for her support and ideas about this article. I also appreciate myself for asking!

Recommended Reading

Satir, Virginia, John Banmen, Jane Gerber, Maria Gomori

1991   The Satir Model: Family Therapy and Beyond.

Satir and her colleagues wrote this compilation of her ideas and therapeutic techniques, along with the theory and beliefs behind them. The book describes her "Stages of Change" (p.98-119). All you have to do is replace the word "family" with "person," and you'll discover the universality of the model.

CHAPTER 14
What Instructors Are Paid For, or The ABCs of Fee-Setting

I had an eye-opening experience the other day. At the end of a private lesson, my student handed me a few bills to pay my fee. And then she pulled another bill out of her wallet and pushed it into my hand. "I should pay you more," she said. "You saved my life!" I did some mumbling, tried to refuse the extra money, and then finally took it as she went on praising me to the heavens.

If I had blushing genes, my face would have been magenta. All my old issues about getting paid for my work surged into consciousness. Had I really earned the extra money? Was this about the quality of my work or the depths of her previous despair? Should I even get paid at all for doing something I love so much?

When I related this incident to a friend and colleague, she said: "Nonsense! This just means you're not charging enough." (Sound effects here: the whoosh of old issues surging up to consciousness again.)

Those old issues have been a lifelong challenge for me. It's a measure of how far I've come in meeting and vanquishing the challenge that I can write about this. I know I'm not alone. Many of us in this profession struggle with these issues day after day. Women in particular. Why? As psychologists are discovering,

137

men usually accept their successes as real, whereas women often seem to need to keep proving themselves. For a woman, a success is not a success but a fluke, an accident. And, unfortunately for many of us women, there will never be enough positive and incontrovertible proof of our competence to convince us. The disbelieving and re-proving process goes on and on. And yet, as prevalent as these feelings are, this is one of those things that nobody talks about.

The core issue, I believe, is a temporary crisis of self-esteem. The core question is: Am I worthy? If I'm not sure about my worth, how can I dare bring up this discussion? What if I'm right? What if my friend had said: "Your student was just feeling relief, after a long spell of desperation. You're really a miserable instructor, and she'd have known that if she'd just returned to a sane and rational state of mind. In fact, she probably has figured that out by now, and I'd be surprised if she ever called you again."

Talk about nightmares!

Once I had calmed down and really heard my friend's actual words ("You're not charging enough."), I began to think about what exactly my students are paying for. Instead of focusing on how much I'm getting, I started thinking about how much they're getting. Many students are unclear as to just what they get in return for my fee. This is not surprising, as my fees cover a wide range of intangibles. That's why I've decided to break out some of the components, in simple ABC format. Next time someone asks how much I charge, I'll remember what they're getting—and reply without doubt or embarrassment.

A for Attention

I suspect my students would be astonished to discover how much time I spend thinking about them and their problems when

I'm not "at work." I might be hiking in the woods, or reading a magazine, or taking a shower, and a thought comes to me about something that will help a student. For example, I was driving home from a private lesson in Santa Fe last week and suddenly realized that I'd spent the whole hour working out a training plan for a new student with a dog that wouldn't enter his crate. I could have been enjoying the enchanting scenery—and maybe I was. But most of my conscious mind was focused on dogs and crates, developing the plan. Supper had to wait until I had worked out the details on my computer.

And that's just conscious attention. I don't know about you, but I often dream about my students' problems, awakening in the middle of the night with solution ideas. This happens so frequently, I keep paper and pencil handy on my night table, where I've mounted a high-intensity lamp that won't awaken my husband when I'm scribbling away at three in the morning.

B for Behavior

No matter what a student brings to the class or private lesson, they are sure to leave with a better understanding of canine behavior. Just yesterday, a student with an 8-month-old Sheltie learned that when a dog yawns, he's not bored. And, along with the yawn, sweaty paw prints on the floor of the training room tell us that he's worried, stressed, or maybe just plain tired—and we need to take a break.

C for not Clock-Watching

My friend, Lee Livingood, says this succinctly: *"I deliberately keep my client base small so I can give personal attention. I charge for an hour-long session, but the session is more like an hour and a half."*

I spent many years teaching at a university. People working in that system believe that all subjects can be taught (and, presumably, learned) in exactly 14 weeks, in 50-minute "training periods," three times a week. I knew then that this was absurd. It's even more absurd when we're teaching two students at a time, the dog and the handler. And even more so when we realize that one of those students doesn't even speak English!

Of course, there's a built-in trap here. I can become really sloppy and inefficient by telling myself that a private lesson or a class can take as much time as we need. But, on the other hand, I can also become a robot that stops teaching when the bell rings! Somewhere in the middle, there's a region of professionalism coupled with self-knowledge. I freely admit that things take longer when I'm teaching than they do when some of my colleagues are teaching. And this means that I need to be a self-watcher—not a clock-watcher—to keep myself on track.

D for Dedication

My students unconsciously expect me to be on call, not only for the planned lessons or classes, but also for unexpected emergencies, incidental questions, idle speculation, and all sorts of administrative work such as rescheduling at their convenience. Moreover, I get neither sick days nor vacation days. When I say I'll be there—and sometimes even when I haven't said—I'm there. Even when I'm not there, I've implicitly or explicitly restricted my other activities so I'll be able to respond to their needs in a reasonable time.

E for Experience

Most of my students have had, at most, a handful of dogs in their lives. I've known, observed, interacted with, and helped to train hundreds. I bring that experience to my teaching, and it helps me to generalize (carefully!) about such things as what is

140

"normal," what characteristics are breed-specific or age-related, what behaviors might be medical in origin, and so on.

So, for example, when a student worries that her 10-week-old puppy is "aggressive" because the puppy "bites," I can put her mind at ease about the features of normal puppy behavior. Only when her expectations are more realistic can we talk about strategies to reduce the mouthing. Or when an older dog suddenly begins to take exception to the approaches of another household dog, I can suggest that it might be time for a thorough veterinary checkup. Or when a dog suddenly starts house soiling, after years of being housetrained, I can investigate what changes have happened in the household that might be contributing to this.

F for Flexibility

What I offer students is a philosophy and a set of guiding principles. Within that framework, though, what I give them is specific methods and techniques that actually work for them and their dogs. As an operant trainer, I want the dog to drive the learning process. But as a tactical instructor, I know that there are many ways to arrange for a dog to "offer" a Down that I can reinforce. If one way doesn't work, then I dig into my grab bag of techniques until I find one that does.

I once knew an instructor who followed an implicit philosophy of training that was never articulated (probably not even in her own mind). What she gave her students was just a cookbook of methods. If a particular method didn't seem to be working, it must be someone's fault—never the instructor or the method. Either the student was not doing it right, or the dog was somehow deficient. If this instructor didn't know how to solve a problem, she declared it insoluble. For example, she once told a student that his dog's fear of vacuum cleaners was just something he had to live with "because it was a phobia."

H for Honesty

The work I do for my clients can sometimes literally mean the life or death of a beloved pet. This is a grave responsibility, and I accept it fully and do whatever is necessary to give full value. If I don't know how to solve a problem, I say so and refer the student to someone else who can help. If I believe that the problem cannot be solved in the present circumstances, I don't hesitate to tell the student. And if those circumstances can't be changed, then I might suggest rehoming the dog into a situation that will be happier for all concerned.

K for Knowledge

My students don't pay directly for all the education I bring to the job—not just my formal education, but, for example, the thousands of hours I spend reading and studying videos in my own and related fields. I figure that in a typical year, I read the equivalent of two books a week, perhaps more. Very few of my day-job friends devote this kind of personal time to their own development. And, when they take a seminar or attend a conference, their employer pays for them—but not for me.

O for Overhead

Although I may charge students for out-of-pocket costs, such as transportation, I don't charge for meals, supplies, reasonable phone calls, faxes, mailing, and so forth. All these expenses are lumped into my fees, along with with my other overhead—my own office and training space, utility bills, computers, software, insurance, business cards and letterheads, and professional development.

Most instructors are paid by the hour or for a class. This method of payment tends to emphasize a single tangible component of what my students are getting—my actual, physical presence. It does not take into account all the backstage and behind-the-scenes expenses that make my teaching possible.

U for Understanding

I am most definitely not a psychotherapist, but many of my students have said that I have helped them in ways that go far beyond the specifics of training a dog. I understand that, in American culture, dogs are regarded as family members—usually, as children. This means that dogs are part of the dynamic family system. So, for example, when a husband and wife are in conflict, the dog may well become the focus and lightning rod of their struggle.

The family dog can serve as what psychologists call the "identified patient." In these cases, everything that happens is "the dog's fault." Or the dog becomes the victim or the tormentor of one of the spouses. It may be much easier to cloak the dog in these guises than it is for the couple to face the real issues between them.

All of us have stories like this in our case files. There's the one about the stay-at-home mom with 4 preschool-age children, whose husband has brought home a dog—"for the kids." Now this mom gets to have a fifth "child" to deal with, while the husband pursues his career, works late at the office, and goes on out-of-town business trips every other week. Furthermore, the last time the husband brought home a dog, the dog bit their then-two-year-old child and they "got rid of him" (the dog, not the husband). I earned my fee by encouraging this woman to bring the new dog to my beginners' class, and by staying with her until she began to see that she really could handle the situation and that this would not be another disposable dog in their lives.

And there's the story of the woman who is a compulsive "rescuer"—and the creatures she rescues are dogs. She's just brought home her sixth "abused dog", without her husband's approval or participation, and calls me tearfully to say that her marriage is now coming apart at the seams. What should she do? I earned my fee by listening with understanding and empathy until she was able to make her own decision—one that she could live with.

What about the rest of the ABCs? I'm sure I could find something my students get from me for each letter of the alphabet. Yes, even Z! How about ZZZZZ for sleep? That's something that all of us need in order to give our students our best—and something that we're not directly paid for.

Once again, I turn to my friend Lee's own words: *"It took me a long time to get past the idea that I had to be "affordable" or that I shouldn't charge too much because I wasn't The Expert. I still sometimes struggle with those issues of value, but I'm getting there. I may not be The Expert but I'm a whole lot better than most of the others around.*

"I do no advertising. Everything is by vet referral or word of mouth. I've finally figured out that service and commitment are what I really charge for. I offer senior discounts, discounts to people who adopt rescues, discounts for (you name it).

"I find ways to justify a discount if I think cost is the only thing that is preventing someone who is truly committed from doing what they can to help their dog.

"Am I going to get rich like this? Since I can't work at this full time, am I even going to pay the mortgage? Heck, no! But I sleep well—that is, when I'm not busy worrying about my clients and their dogs, and whether or not I did everything perfectly."

And there it is again—the struggle we all face about having to prove our own worth, every time. Maybe it's time for all of us to write our own ABCs of Fee-Setting so that we can remind ourselves of what we're really being paid for.

My deep appreciation to my husband, Jerry Weinberg, who inspired this chapter and has helped me through my own struggles.

CHAPTER 15
My Year as a Seminar Junkie

"Every once in a while, I have to be a student again—so that I don't forget what it's like."

That's what my trainer friend Sally told me as she handed me her registration form for my class. And that's just one of the many reasons I admire her.

Any instructor who feels she has nothing new to learn is just kidding herself and probably short-changing her students.

The year 2000 was, for me, much more than just the turn of the century. It was the year I had chosen to be a student again. During that year, I attended ten seminars, including some on dog training and others on training animals of all kinds. A couple of these were at home, but all the others were out of town, an airplane (or two) trip away. My husband remarked that, for someone who hates to travel, I sure was doing a lot of travelling! I learned a lot about training dogs, but, maybe even more important, I learned a lot about what it's like to sit on the other side of the desk and be a student. I myself teach seminars only occasionally, but all of these learnings will contribute to my being a better class instructor.

When Does the Class Begin?

The class begins when the student first thinks about it. Every week, I receive several inquiries about my classes and private training. Each one is prompted by a need or a desire on the part of the prospective student. For example, someone sent me an email recently outlining her dog's behavior problems. After a long and insightful description, she wrote: *"I am told dog trainers can help, and I'm interested."* The "I am told" part of the statement suggests that this was a new idea for her. But even before writing this statement, she had titled her post "Dog Training," demonstrating that she was already thinking about this as a possible solution to her problems. That was the moment when the class began for her. And that's the moment when we can begin to set realistic and positive expectations for the student.

One of the seminars I attended this year had a different beginning moment for me. It happened when the presenter sent out an email to everyone who was enrolled, asking us to send her a Wish List answering the following questions:

1. What do you like best about your dog?
2. What are your hopes/plans for your dog?
3. What have you done with your dog so far?
4. What would you like to change about your dog or your relationship?
5. What else would you like to say?

As I read these questions, I realized that this was not going to be a one-size-fits-all seminar but one tailored to my needs and wishes. The seminar presenter cared about me and my dog and wanted enough information to satisfy our needs. With that expectation, I went to the seminar feeling safe, cared for, and open to learning. And, even better, as I answered the questions, I gained some insights that probably would not have come without the act of thinking about and writing out my answers. So the seminar learnings began for me long before the actual seminar began.

In sharp contrast, another seminar presenter sent information to prospective participants that included pages and pages about his philosophy, his background and experience, and a "thumbnail sketch" of his life story. Buried somewhere in all this material was the logistical information I needed to decide if I wanted to go— the where, when, and how much. It turned out to be a marvelous seminar that had a huge influence on my work, but it started out as a quagmire of verbiage that meant little to me at the time. The moment I arrived at the seminar I realized that this was going to be anything but a quagmire. Instead, the seminar was a very clear, practical, hands-on learning experience that would have immediate applications to my work. I had to make a quick shift in my expectations. Why make things that difficult? Learning is hard enough! And, if I had let myself get lost in the quagmire of information, I might not even have gone to this wonderful seminar.

One way that I've brought these learnings about setting expectations into my own teaching is by including the following question on my class registration form: *"What do you like best about your dog?"* While the other questions on the form are designed to give me information—about the dog and about the owner's past experience with dogs and training—this question is really intended as the beginning of the class for the student.

What I'm really saying when I ask this question is that effective training starts with a positive attitude. The question assumes that the owner does like something about the dog, regardless of any problems he would like to solve. (There's a separate question on the form: *"What do you want to accomplish in this class?"*) I want my students to start by seeing their dogs as likeable. I want them to come to class with the positive attitudes that translate into hope. I want them to expect that they'll enjoy the class and that their dogs are really capable of learning.

Creature Comforts

One of my unconscious expectations for a seminar is that the physical environment will not interfere with my learning. I take for granted certain things like air temperature, acoustics, and adequate working space for me and my dog.

I became aware of these expectations at a few of the seminars I attended this year. One of them was held in an enormous barn-like building at the local fairground. It was so cold that I couldn't take my coat off for most of the two days. And the sound bounced back and forth from wall to wall to ceiling so that I could hardly hear the speaker. She tried to remedy this by using a PA system, but that only made things worse. Now the sounds bouncing around the building were simply louder and even more jarring.

Another seminar I attended was held in a city hotel. I've taught enough seminars to know that most hotels are totally unsuited for learning. They might work for weddings or for stand-up lectures, but they certainly don't work for experiential learning situations in which the students are expected to talk to each other, listen to each other, move around, and manipulate animals or objects. I can live with spending a week in a room without windows. I can even live with the typically uncomfortable hotel chairs. But, at this seminar, I discovered my threshold of tolerance.

In this hotel meeting room, our choices were simple: we could either hear ourselves think, or we could melt from the heat. The air-conditioning system was not working well, they told us. My own suspicion is that it was just a poorly designed system. When it became too hot to bear, we turned on the air-conditioning which blasted noisily in the fairly small room. When we could no longer stand the strain on our ears and brains, we turned it off. This cycle continued for 5 days, and many of us spent an inordinate amount of time near the coffee urn in the hall outside our meeting room, where it was cooler and quieter.

I can now better appreciate my own students' needs for the creature comfort of reasonable air temperature. My training room is what I like to call an "indoor-outdoor" room. The only heating is provided by 3 small electric heaters strategically attached to the walls. When I'm teaching, I rarely feel cold, but I realize that my students come in different shapes and sizes and temperature sensitivities. So I tell them on the first day of class to dress in layers—and I try to keep them moving! In the summer, my training room becomes an oven and even I can't stand it then. So I've completely given up holding classes at that time of year.

The physical environment should be completely transparent to teacher and students. When everything is right, we shouldn't even notice it. When we do start to notice it, that awareness definitely gets in the way of learning.

Class Size

I worry sometimes when my class is smaller than usual—smaller than my own hopes and expectations specify. My training-room capacity is 8 dog/handler teams. In order to make sure I reach capacity, I could over-enroll the class. I dare not do that, though, because, most of the time, all the teams who sign up actually do take the class. Every now and then, however, someone has to drop out—sometimes even before the class begins but when it's too late to fill the space.

This past winter, for example, I had enrolled 6 teams and was looking forward to an especially fine class consisting of some serious students. Three of them dropped out before the first class meeting because of family or health crises, and one more dropped after the first week when she realized that she would have to do some work on her own. I was suddenly left with a class of two. I could not bring myself to cancel the class and disappoint those two people who had, after all, stayed with it. And I didn't think of any other solutions until much later—for example, running the class as a series of semiprivate sessions and holding fewer of them. So I went through with it and wondered, each week, what these two students thought and what it was like for them to be in a sub-optimally-sized class. It was only at the last class meeting that I dared to ask them. What a surprise to hear that they had loved being in such a small class and getting all that extra, personalized attention!

I had a chance to experience the same thing when one of the seminars I attended turned out to have only three people in it. The enrollment limit was 10 and, at one time, there were actually 10 enrolled. But as time went on—and life interfered!—the number dropped to three. We three felt especially privileged, and I made sure to tell the instructor who, like me, was a little concerned about what his three students thought about all this.

Yes, it was certainly a different experience. And yes, my preference usually leans towards smaller rather than larger classes. And yes again, you do need a certain miminum amount of energy for a class to work well. What I learned, though, was that there were also some distinct benefits to a "too small" class. If this ever happens again in one of my own classes, I'll have a different view of it, and I'll also have some ideas about how to make this work instead of just mindlessly plodding through.

Structure

I confess! I like structure! That is, as long as I can get around it and do things my own way.

One of the seminars I attended was highly structured—and with good reason. Part of what we were learning about was gathering, recording, and analyzing data. We worked in very brief time segments, ranging from 1 to 5 minutes each. In addition, we were supposed to divide the longer time segments into several shorter ones. So, for example, we might work for 4 minutes total, 1 minute at a time, and then spend the fifth minute doing our planning for the next 5-minute segment. We would repeat this cycle for a total of about 45 minutes in a single session. Each seminar participant had access to a kitchen timer, so that we could keep track. So for the entire 45- minute session, timers were beeping around us almost constantly. Sometimes, it was even difficult to know if this was my timer or my neighbor's.

I didn't mind the beeping so much, since I'm pretty good at blocking out extraneous sounds. What I did mind, though, was being put on a schedule that didn't always fit for me. There were times when I wanted to violate the 1-minute-at-a-time rule, and so I did. It may be that I lost some valuable learning in the process, but it's more likely that, by taking matters into my own hands, I maximized my learning. Instead of getting angry, I took action based on self-knowledge, knowing how I learn best.

I doubt that the seminar presenter had this in mind when she designed the structure or even that she noticed that I and probably others were violating that structure. What's important here is that I was sharply reminded of the need to provide a structure and also to allow for deviations from that structure. I try to remember this when I design my own classes, by making room for and respecting individual differences among my students. I also need to keep clearly in mind my own bottom line. If it's essential to the learning goals for students to follow the suggested structure exactly, I tell them so. If it's not, then I offer them alternatives.

For example, the homework instructions for Week 2 in my beginners' class specify exactly how many minutes the student should work on each exercise each day. Because we're building the basic mechanical skills of training, it's important that students practice each one carefully. I even ask them to use a kitchen timer to make sure they follow the instructions to the letter. Once I started doing this, I was delighted to see that their skills developed quickly, and they were pleased to see the effects on their dog's progress. In later weeks, though, such precise, minute-by-minute homework instructions are less critical, and I allow for variations in the students' schedules and personal styles by suggesting, for example, that they do "3-5 training sessions" on this exercise, or that they work on another "at least once a day."

After the first few weeks of class, prescribed structure begins to be replaced by an understanding of principles. Students can then use their understanding to guide them as they plan their training schedules. By this time, they realize that, as one of my own teachers said, no single training session will make or break the learning process. And sometimes, a break in structure—for example, when a student has to go out of town for a week—can actually be a good thing. Both handler and dog return to training refreshed and ready to work again.

Realistic Goal Setting

Setting goals for students is a good thing to do at the beginning of the class, but those goals must be achievable. On the first day of one of the seminars I attended, the instructor laid out for us what we were supposed to accomplish with our animal by the end of the seminar. He described one of the goals:

 a. The animal must pull a receptacle,
 b. with a certain minimum weight in it,
 c. for a specified distance.

Not a single person accomplished this goal. And, as we moved through the five days of the seminar, the goal was never again mentioned. I don't have any idea if this goal had ever been met in past offerings of this seminar, or if this was just the instructor's vision of an ideal—something to strive for but probably never achieve. What I do know is that we felt increasingly frustrated as the days went by when we saw that our animals would never make it.

In my own classes, I do not set or state such specific goals. I don't promise that the dogs will, for example, be able to do 30-second Down-Stays by the end of the class. Instead, I state goals in much more general terms—and, more often, as hopes. For example, I tell my students that my own objectives are to help them become better trainers, and to build stronger relationships with their dogs. I also explain that each dog is an individual, and I encourage students to pay attention to all the feedback they receive from their dogs that will help them set—and meet—realistic expectations.

In another seminar I attended, the instructor not only stated goals that might never be met, but she also told us about former seminar participants who had far exceeded those goals. I suppose she was trying to motivate us, but the effect of her words was just the opposite. That's one of the reasons that I don't use my own well-trained dog to demonstrate behaviors in my beginners' classes. Although this is usually fun to watch, many students find it really discouraging—especially when they learn that I've been training my own dog for several years now. I would much rather have them see one of their own classmates demonstrate something new that the dog actually gets very quickly. "I can do that!" is the implicit message.

Partnering Can Be Difficult

I like to build friendly and collaborative relationships among my students. And I like to have them play the role of Coach as well as Student. So for years I have divided my classes into smaller work groups—sometimes two's, sometimes three's—for some of the class activities.

It's true that we can learn something from just about any partner. Sometimes, though, partnering can get in the way of learning. In one seminar I attended, for example, the instructor paired us by simply counting off. We were supposed to take turns at training a certain behavior in our dogs and giving each other feedback. I was partnered with a woman whose only comment on my training efforts was "Cool!" And when I tried to give her feedback on what I was seeing when it was her turn to train, she just said "Mmmm." I have no idea if she even heard what I was saying. I do know, though, that this was one of the most frustrating attempts at communication that I've ever experienced. Fortunately, it lasted only for a few minutes. In another seminar, we were supposed to choose a partner to work with throughout the entire week. We were told not to choose someone we already knew. Why? The seminar instructor believed that partnering could destroy a friendship or work relationship. Some people ignored the rule, having already made arrangements in advance to work with a friend or colleague. The remaining partnerships were formed very quickly—and I was not quick enough. Within just a few minutes, there were only two of us left. That meant that we would be partners!

I silently reminded myself of my belief that I could learn something from any partner. And that belief carried me through the seminar. My partner was about as different from me in style, values, rhythm, and general feelings about life as he could possibly be. And I'm sure he felt the same way about me. We did manage to have a reasonably good working relationship, and we certainly did learn a lot from each other. So maybe it was a good thing after all, even though part of me felt some irritation at having this extra burden.

In the past, I never paid much attention to how I formed partnerships in my own classes, but, after having these experiences in the seminars I attended, I'm going to pay a lot more attention in the future—especially when the partnership is going to be of fairly long duration (more than 1 hour). In that case, I would arrange for students to become somewhat acquainted before asking them to commit to a partnership.

I have several ways of doing this, depending on the amount of time I can allow for the process. For example, I've had students mill around in the room, stopping to talk to every other student briefly and ask a few simple questions that I suggest—"What brings you to this class?" or "What's your number-one goal for your dog?" or some other more seminar-specific question. Or I might have each student briefly introduce herself and her dog to the entire class, telling us something about the student's occupation, training experience, and any special needs or wishes she has for herself and her dog.

Sometimes, I ask my students to think about what they want in a partner and what they can offer. Then they write this up on a large sheet of paper. We post all the sheets on the wall for everyone to read, and then the partnerships can be negotiated. I also ask people to decide, before they make their choices, if they'd learn more by partnering with someone like them or very different from them.

Positive Reinforcement and Competition

Something I learned—again—in one of the seminars I attended was that I like positive reinforcement, but I don't like to compete for it. A "Good job!" does a lot for me and my learning. But having more "Good jobs!" than someone else is not only irrelevant but creates a negative learning environment for me.

I have never much cared for positive reinforcement in the form of tangible tokens. When instructors do this, they expect students to accumulate the tokens in order to win prizes at the end of the class. So the tokens become currency, and their reinforcement value is diluted.

This became very clear to me in one of the seminars I attended. The instructor walked around, observing us at work, and stopped now and then to give positive reinforcement to a participant in the form of a verbal "Good job!" and a poker chip. On the last day of the seminar, we were to count up how many poker chips we had received—and now they were no longer positive reinforcers but just poker chips—and then exchange them for prizes, based on the numbers. So if I had the greatest number of poker chips, I got the best prize. I was very uncomfortable through this process, and a few of my classmates simply refused to participate.

In contrast, one of my most memorable moments in a different seminar I attended was when I absolutely glowed at receiving a verbal positive reinforcer. This was a seminar about operant conditioning, and we were working with chickens. My partner's chicken had panicked, jumped off the training table, and was wandering around the room, clucking wildly in distress. We needed to recapture the chicken and get back to training.

157

My partner slowly approached her from the front with food. I came up behind the chicken very slowly and, with balletic grace, I smoothly reached out at just the right moment and grasped her firmly with both hands. The instructor had watched this entire scene as it played out in slow motion. As I triumphantly picked up the animal, the instructor said "Nice catch!" His words meant more to me than any poker chip, and I still grin at the memory.

Vulnerability

At some of the seminars I attended, I surprised myself at how sensitive and vulnerable I can be. When one instructor singled out a participant for public praise and said not a word about any of the others, I wilted. I was tom between uncertainty and anger. Was this the only person who had done a good job on this assignment? Were the rest of us sadly lacking in skill? The anger came from wondering why my own efforts had not been at least acknowledged.

At another seminar, I found myself and my dog "on stage" to demonstrate 30 seconds of attention. I had volunteered for the job by raising my hand when the instructor asked if anyone had a dog who could do this. I thought I had such a dog. To my surprise and chagrin, my dog was a dismal failure, and I stood there feeling foolish and very vulnerable at that moment. As it turned out, that was one of the most important learnings I took from the seminar—the fact that my dog did not have the ability to hold focus in a very distracting environment. 1 might not have appreciated this fact, if I had been less sensitive. As it is, though, I remember the moment—and my feelings—well. Emotionally charged moments like this may be unpleasant but they certainly leave a lasting impression.

In my own classes, I like to have students demonstrate individually in front of the whole group. But instead of asking for finished performance, I use these demonstrations to show how to start teaching a new behavior. It's almost implicit, then, that the demonstrating team will be awkward and have problems. That takes away some of the potential for vulnerability. And sometimes the team does so well that they get extra reinforcement from all of us.

What Do Students Learn?

In the seminars I attended, what I learned wasn't always what the teacher thought he or she was teaching. Instead, I learned what I needed and was ready to learn. And I'm absolutely sure that's true for every student, in every seminar or class.

In the 1970s, when I started my formal teaching career at the university, one of the buzzwords was Relevance. The idea was that if there was no perceived value or utility to the learning (from the student's point of view), then it just wouldn't happen. I'm afraid that remains true today, even though the buzzwords may have changed.

So, for example, insisting that my beginning students have their dogs in perfect Heel position as they're strolling through the park is one of those Relevance issues. Who cares about perfect position? Most of my beginning students don't! What they want is a dog that doesn't pull on the leash.

In my advanced class, I teach Scent Discrimination, and my students love the challenge and the fun of it. If I offered this to my beginning students, they would be completely baffled. Why, they would ask, are we doing this? And I really would not have an answer for them.

But when we work on environmental (instead of verbal) cues for Sit, in my beginners' class, it's immediately clear to them why we're doing this. Do you want your dog to dash out the door when you open it and get hit by a passing truck, before you've had time to say "Sit"? Of course not. That's why you teach your dog to sit and wait automatically, without being asked to, as you open the door. One of my students took this a delightful step further and taught her excited dog to sit at the sight of the leash in her hand. So now, instead of having to wrestle her dog to put on the leash for a walk, she and her dog both could enjoy the walk from the very beginning.

People who study learning sometimes talk about the "10% Rule." They tell us that, on average, students get only 10% of what we're teaching on their first exposure to new material. And, to make matters worse, different students in a class get different pieces that amount to their own 10%. We all know that repeating new ideas in various ways helps people learn. That's just an application of the 10% Rule. I was lucky enough to experience this in myself at one of the seminars I attended. Here are my notes for that session:

"Marsha (the instructor) gave us a very clear answer to my request for information about why eating and stress are "antagonistic" (in learning-theory terminology). A good example for humans is this: you're eating dinner with the family and suddenly a big argument starts between 2 family members. You "lose your appetite." That's because there are 2 separate sub-systems within the Peripheral/Autonomic Nervous System—the Sympathetic and the Parasympathetic. The Sympathetic is about expending energy, and the Parasympathetic about conserving energy. Expending energy might take the form of physical activity, excitement, aggression, fight-or-flight response, etc. Conserving energy is what's going on when we eat, digest food, metabolize food, rest, etc. Only one of these subsystems can be activated at a time."

Got it? I thought I had at the time. It was clear as a bell, as was everything else presented to us in this outstanding seminar. But when I got home and tried to explain it to my own students, I couldn't remember much except that stressed dogs can't eat. And they already knew that! So I applied the 10% Rule and reread my notes a number of times before my next class meeting. Then I was able to give my students a much fuller explanation of how this works. But I still have trouble remembering which part of the Nervous System does what!

After having this experience myself, I'm much more tolerant of my students when they don't get something, even after I'm sure I've presented it very clearly. Instead of getting annoyed, I simply apply the 10% Rule and find other ways to say the same thing—until they've heard it enough times, in enough different ways, so that they can really take it in.

When my year as a seminar junkie ended, I had lots of rich memories and a stack of folders filled with notes I took during all these seminars. Notes like this one have been especially helpful to me as I teach my own classes:

"Now I know how my beginning students must feel the first night of class!!!"

This was a year filled with learnings—not only about the subject matter of the seminars but, more importantly, about the learning process itself. I believe that my own students have benefited on both counts. I can pass on to them the new information and ideas that I learned, and I can also make their learning smoother and easier by knowing what it's like to be walking in their mocassins.

A Final Word

If you've benefited from this book by reading about my experiences, then I'm content. Better yet, if you've been inspired to try some of the new ideas you've read about and to continue learning more about yourself and your human students, then I'm ecstatic.

I'd love to hear more about your experiences. I also welcome your comments and suggestions. All of these will contribute to my own continued growth and development as an instructor. You can reach me by email at: <daniw3@comcast.net>

READINGS AND OTHER RESOURCES

READINGS AND OTHER RESOURCES

In 1986, Job Michael Evans wrote, in his Foreword to Volhard and Fisher's Teaching Dog Obedience Classes:

"There is a new wave of canine professionals in America today who place equal emphasis on dog and owner.... In my opinion, we will never change the way dogs are treated in our society unless we change the way we instruct their owners."

We may not agree with all the dog-training methods advocated in these books, but we do need to honor the authors as pioneers – the first to suggest that instructors also need to pay attention to the human end of the leash.

PIONEERING BOOKS

Pryor, Karen

 1999 Don't Shoot the Dog: The New Art of Teaching and Training.

This is the book that started it all! First published in 1984, this revised edition includes a chapter on clicker training - "A New Technology." Even though the book is over 20 years old, it's still very worth reading. It's a true classic.

Evans, Job Michael

 1985 The Evans Guide for Counseling Dog Owners.

This book is about what Evans calls "technique" – such as, how to get started, doing good inter-views, dealing with all kinds of people, working with problem behaviors, collaborating with veterinarians, and setting fees. In his chapter about "Characteristics of Dog Owners," he applies Virginia Satir's communication model very effectively. This book has aged well, even though the training methods of its time have been superseded. And the illustrations by Carol Lea Benjamin, another dog trainer, are a real treat.

1995   Training and Explaining: How to be the Dog Trainer You Want to Be.

The last book published by the late, famous dog trainer who also co-authored the first book by the Monks of New Skete (How To Be Your Dog's Best Friend). Evans was a traditional trainer, much loved in the dog-training community. This book is his legacy and includes chapters on many topics of interest to trainers and instructors.

Volhard, Joachim and Gail Tamases Fisher
1986   Teaching Dog Obedience Classes: The Manual for Instructors.

These authors collaborated on a dog-training book three years earlier. Their training approach was called the "Motivational Method," reflecting the beginning of the shift to less compulsive training. In this book, they focus on the instructor and the human student. About 10 years later, Gail Fisher "crossed over" to clicker training and, in 2009, published The Thinking Dog - Crossover to Clicker Training.

MODERN BOOKS

Donaldson, Jean
1996   The Culture Clash.

A ground-breaking book by an outstanding dog trainer. Donaldson makes a powerful case for thinking in terms of behavior rather than the older and more anthropomorphic dominance models of dog training.

Clothier, Suzanne
    2002   Bones Would Rain from the Sky.
This is not a how-to training manual but a book about deepening our relationships with dogs. Clothier goes far beyond the mechanical aspects of living with and training dogs and explores how to build connection without force or coercion.

McConnell, Patricia, Ph.D.
    2002   The Other End of the Leash.
McConnell, an Applied Animal Behaviorist and long-time dog trainer and dog owner, has written a beautiful and very personal book filled with wisdom about how to live with and train dogs. A lot of the book is about how we humans, as primates, are different from and the same as canines, with lots of good information about how to make the best use of this understanding to build better relationships with our dogs.

Alexander, Melissa
    2003   Click For Joy!
This is an excellent book for anyone interested in doing clicker training. Alexander is true to the method, explaining the pitfalls of other training techniques including some that are "positive" but less effective than clicker training. I recommend this book to beginning trainers and to new dog owners.

Yin, Sophia, D.V.M.
    2004   How To Behave So Your Dog Behaves.
A very user-friendly explanation of the science of how animals

learn, written with clarity and humor by an applied animal behaviorist and veterinarian. Includes detailed applications of the scientific principles to training basic behaviors and solving common behavior problems.

Wilde, Nicole

    2004   One On One: A Dog Trainer's Guide to Private Training.

    2003   It's Not the Dogs, It's the People! A Dog Trainer's Guide to Training Humans.

    2001   So You Want to be a Dog Trainer.
All three of these small books are well worth reading, especially if you're new at instructing.

Ryan, Terry

    2005   Coaching People to Train Their Dogs
Just about everything you need to know to be an effective instructor. This book will be useful for beginning instructors as well as for the more experienced. Ryan has put together, in this one very readable volume, a complete range of topics, from the practical and concrete to the theoretical backdrop.

McDevitt, Leslie

    2007   Control Unleashed: Creating a Focused and Confident Dog.

If you have a dog who is "over the top" around excitement or distraction, this is the book for you. Specially written for Agility people but extremely useful for anyone who wants a positive approach to helping a dog relax, focus, and work off leash reliably – even in the excitement of an Agility class or trial. The book is also very helpful for counterconditioning a reactive dog who is easily stressed and lacking in confidence.

Dodds, W. Jean, DVM and Diana R. Laverdure
    2011   The Canine Thyroid Epidemic: Answers You Need for Your Dog.
    An excellent resource for dog owners to help you understand the frequently under diagnosed disease of hypothyroidism. You might want to share it with your veterinarian.

ON THE INTERNET

Dog Aware
www.dogaware.com
    Well researched and current information about nutrition, health, etc.

Karen Pryor
www.clickertraining.com
    Excellent information, articles, video clips, books, videos, equipment for clicker training.

Sophia Yin, DVM
www.drsophiayin.com
    The website of the world-famous, late behaviorist and teacher now maintained by her colleagues. Full of useful information.

Linda P. Case, M.S.
www.TheScienceDog.wordpress.com
    The marvelous blog written by Linda Case, a canine/feline nutritionist, trainer, behavior consultant, author of several excellent books.

Eileen and Dogs
www.EileenandDogs.com
The blog written by Eileen, a highly respected, amateur dog trainer and writer.

PROFESSIONAL ORGANIZATIONS

Association of Pet Dog Trainers (APDT)
http://apdt.com

International Association of Animal Behavior Consultants (IAABC)
http://www.iaabc.org

National Association of Dog Obedience Instructors (NADOI)
http://www.nadoi.org

Pet Professional Guild
https://www.petprofessionalguild.com

DANI WEINBERG, PHD, CDBC

Dani Weinberg is a dog trainer, behavior consultant, and trainers' trainer through her business Dogs & Their People. Formerly a university professor with a Ph.D. in Anthropology, her current professional life in the world of dogs allows her to pursue her lifelong interests in learning and communication.

Originally trained in traditional methods that used "corrections," Dani has switched entirely to operant/clicker training. She's been doing this for almost 30 years, and she's still learning! For 9 of those years, she was a Faculty member of the Karen Pryor Academy - a highly regarded professional dog training program. Dani is also a Certified Dog Behavior Consultant through the International Association of Dog Behavior Consultants.

Dani has taught beginners' and advanced classes, puppy classes, post-adoption classes, and classes for puppy raisers for an assistance-dog organization. She has also presented seminars on a wide variety of dog-related topics. For the past 20 years, she's been concentrating on private training and in-home behavior consultation.

One of her long time passions is working as a volunteer with the Warm Hearts Network - a program that registers human-dog teams to visit schools, hospitals, and nursing homes - ever since it was formed in 1991.

Over the years, Dani and her German Shepherds have earned titles in AKC Obedience, Tracking, and Herding. They have lived in Albuquerque, New Mexico since 1992.

For more information and some wonderful photos, please visit Dani's website:

www.daniweinberg.com

Made in United States
North Haven, CT
29 April 2024

51925004R00098